WRITING REVIEWS
for READERS' ADVISORY

OTHER BOOKLIST PUBLICATIONS

*Reid's Read-Alouds: Selections
for Children and Teens,* by Rob Reid

The Back Page, by Bill Ott

WRITING REVIEWS
for
READERS' ADVISORY

BRAD HOOPER

AMERICAN LIBRARY ASSOCIATION

Chicago   2010

Brad Hooper, Adult Books Editor at *Booklist*, the review journal for public and school librarians published in Chicago by the American Library Association, is responsible for overseeing the adult book reviewing program at *Booklist*. He has a bachelor of arts in European history and a master of science in library science, both degrees from Eastern Illinois University, and he has done graduate work in European history at the University of Illinois, Urbana-Champaign. He regularly speaks about reviewing to librarian and publisher groups and has conducted review-writing workshops for public librarians across the country. He is the author of *The Short Story Readers' Advisory* (American Library Association, 2000); *The Fiction of Ellen Gilchrist* (Praeger, 2005); *Read On . . . Historical Fiction* (Libraries Unlimited, 2006); and *The Fiction of Alice Munro* (Praeger, 2008).

The paper used in this publication meets the minimum requirements of American National Standard for Information Sciences—Permanence of Paper for Printed Library Materials, ANSI Z39.48-1992.♾

Library of Congress Cataloging-in-Publication Data
Hooper, Brad.
    Writing reviews for readers' advisory / Brad Hooper.
        p.   cm. — (A Booklist publication)
    Includes bibliographical references and index.
    ISBN 978-0-8389-1017-7 (alk. paper)
    1. Book reviewing. 2. Readers' advisory services. I. Title.
    PN98.B7H66 2010
    808'.066028—dc22   2009049528

ISBN-13: 978-0-8389-1017-7

Printed in the United States of America

14   13   12   11   10   5   4   3   2   1

To Brendan Driscoll,
who will always be my buddy.
To Jerry Eberle,
my assistant and great friend.
And to the participants
in my review-writing workshops,
who helped me hone my thoughts
on reviewing.

Book reviewers are the most despicable, loathsome order of swine that ever rooted about the earth. They are sniveling, revolting creatures who feed their own appetites for bile by gnawing apart other people's work.

—Steve Hely, *How I Became a Famous Novelist*

CONTENTS

PREFACE

L et me begin this personal—and, I hope, personable—exploration of the world of reviewing by sharing the nature of my current professional position as well as proposing what you will carry away with you from reading this book.

I am the Adult Books Editor at *Booklist* (the review journal published by the American Library Association in Chicago) but—armed with a bachelor of arts in European history and a master's degree in library science—I began as a full-time book *reviewer* in the Adult Books Department (one of just four staff reviewers). All authors want their books reviewed; reviews sell books. Thus do publishers send their books—published or in galley form—to *Booklist*.

It was a sweet job: I was required to sit at a desk all day and read forthcoming books and write reviews of them. The four of us in the Adult Books Department—the four staff reviewers—had no specialty; we were expected to be well-read generalists, to be able to read, digest, and offer a critique of books on any and all subjects for the general reader. (The target audience for *Booklist* has always been the public and school library.)

All incoming titles for review (*Booklist* is sent pretty much every book published in the United States, most in galley-proof form) were preselected by the Adult Books Editor, which meant that reprints and specialized and academic titles were set aside, and those that indeed fell within our reviewing bailiwick were placed on a "new arrivals" book truck, file cards made for each one by a publishing assistant (for use as a permanent record), and the book truck shown to the four staff reviewers. Today *Booklist* employs several freelance reviewers, most specialists in different genres and topics; back then, all reviewing was done in-house by staff reviewers. The truck of reviewable books was divided into fourths, according to the first letter of the author's last name. Thus, I always got review items whose authors' last names began somewhere between the letter *F* and the letter *K*—a theoretical fourth of the alphabet.

The beneficial aspect of such an arbitrary division is that I learned how to review every kind of book imaginable, from literary fiction to westerns, from history to gardening (and scattered throughout this book are examples of my favorite reviews from over the years). The disadvantage was being locked into the same authors—and locked away from other authors—with no way of acquiring familiarity with those outside my quarter of the alphabet.

The position of staff reviewer was slowly eliminated over the years, evolving into an editorial position that incorporated reviewing but also involved assigning reviews to the growing cadre of freelancers that *Booklist* came to employ—and subsequently editing those reviews. As I had learned how to review books, I then learned how to edit. In both instances, it primarily came down to on-the-job training. I learned to review and then learned to edit, like learning a foreign language, in the best method there is: total immersion in it. Even so, I brought with me to the job three traits that neophyte reviewers might already have and can certainly cultivate: experience in reading books, experience in reading reviews, and experience in writing reviews.

Eventually, I was promoted through the ranks of the Adult Books Department and am now the head of the department.

Just as publishers use reviews to sell books, librarians use reviews to "sell" books, too, to readers looking for an adventure, help in a project, ideas, information, and more. And who better to write reviews for the local newspapers and the library newsletters and websites than librarians? Thus, as Adult Books Editor, I have been asked on numerous occasions to speak to library groups on the topic of reviewing, and I devised a program to help librarians read reviews and write reviews. The first question I am always asked is, How does one get to be a reviewer? There is no degree in reviewing. No "certification" as a reviewer. Further, one does not necessarily need a degree in English, journalism, or creative writing to pursue reviewing. But one can learn to write reviews, and that is what *Writing Reviews for Readers' Advisory* is about.

It really comes down to *experience*. As one of the characters in David Mamet's play *Glengarry, Glen Ross* says, selling real estate is all about location, location, location. As noted above, in reviewing, it's all about experience, experience, experience.

First, experience in reading books. Chances are, a person interested in reviewing, especially a *librarian* interested in reviewing, is someone who has been an avid reader since grammar school. Even if that is the case, read some *more* books. Read widely, too: in other words, not simply in the fields in which you have a keen interest but also in areas to which you would not naturally tend to gravitate.

Second, experience in reading reviews. If you are not an acquisitions librarian, ask those who are to borrow the latest issues of *Booklist, Library Journal,* and *Publishers Weekly* (or search these venues online) to observe the nature—the peculiar slant of the content—of the short, tight reviews found in these sources for prepublication reviews (that is, reviews published before the books themselves are published). Read long reviews in newspapers and magazines to learn the ways in which a longer word count allows the reviewer room to explore the book and its author in more depth.

Third, experience in writing reviews. This experience will be yours to enjoy upon completion of *Writing Reviews for Readers' Advisory* and subsequently delving into writing reviews yourself.

The point of this book, then, is to help readers learn how to look at a book when reviewing it and, just as important, how to look at reviews to learn what a good review's major components are and what reviews should tell you about the book under consideration.

The topic of reviewing young adult and children's books is covered handily in such titles as *From Cover to Cover: Evaluating and Reviewing Children's Books* (Harper, 1997), so this book does not discuss it; nor does this book offer publishers' addresses and the other kinds of information covered so completely by the various writer's-digest-type books.

Finally, audiobook reviewing, a topic of burgeoning importance, is addressed in chapter 8 by librarian par excellence, writer, and audiobook reviewer Joyce Saricks, to whom I give hearty thanks.

Thanks also to Bill Ott, editor and publisher of *Booklist*, for permission to quote extensively from *Booklist* reviews, and to Stephanie Zvirin, acquisitions editor at ALA Editions, who guided me through this project.

MARKETING THROUGH REVIEWING 1

O ne very effective way of marketing your library, of generating interest in using your library's facilities, is to entice readers onto the premises by way of posting, in easily accessed places, reviews of materials recently added to the collection. Simply quoting reviews from other sources, such as *Booklist* and *Library Journal*, will not work; readers can find such blurbs on book jackets and in advertisements. Moreover, such a practice will leave the reader and potential library patron wondering, "Why can't librarians talk about their own books? Just how good *are* these librarians?" And paying outside writers to write reviews for librarians to use on their websites and in other marketing materials can be beyond library budgets.

A few years ago, I attended a Public Library Association conference in Phoenix, Arizona. I sat in on a program presented by a staff person from the Charlotte-Mecklenburg County Library System (in North Carolina). The attractive PowerPoint presentation demonstrated to the audience how a library website can be, and ought to be, set up and maintained. One item presented for discussion was the posting on the website of reviews of new acquisitions, and within that discussion, the program presenter brought up the fact that although staff members wrote these reviews, many staff members did not know how to prepare a review and were thus in need of instruction in how to do so.

The proverbial lightbulb went on above my head, and I had an interesting idea.

After discussion with the *Booklist* editor in chief, Bill Ott, who also thought my idea interesting, I offered on-site instruction, through an announcement made in the pages of *Booklist*, for librarians wanting to learn to write reviews. I developed a two-hour workshop, which I conducted in several libraries throughout the country. This workshop required participants to prepare "mock" reviews in advance; copies of these were sent by the coordinator at the library to all the participants. The workshop itself was broken down in two parts: an hour-long "lecture" on the tenets of reviewing as my experience has informed me (the book you have in your hand derived from this portion of the workshop) and an hour-long discussion by workshop participants of all the reviews that had been submitted. (Find out more about how to conduct such a workshop in your library in chapter 7.)

Reviews written by library staff members are generally produced on either a voluntary basis or as part of their job as readers' advisors, which is the process whereby a librarian leads library patrons from certain books and nonprint materials of which the patron indicated an enjoyment to other books or nonprint materials they are likely to enjoy as well. To volunteer for such a task indicates at least an interest, if not some experience, in review writing. Yet being assigned to write reviews may not indicate an interest in doing so, and if that is the case, it probably indicates a lack of experience, and thus guidance in review writing will be helpful, if not absolutely necessary.

Making the reading and information-seeking public aware of your library is the point, purpose, and thrust of *Writing Reviews for Readers' Advisory*. The path to that public awareness is one that is paved by reviews of the new books and audiobooks that have been accessioned into the library collection. The hoped-for result of such public awareness is to entice readers into the library to become active, satisfied, and returning library patrons. The librarian can make the public aware of these new additions to the library collection via websites, handouts, blogs, book clubs, and so much more.

WEBSITES, HANDOUTS, AND BLOGS

Libraries commonly have websites. Websites have become the most important purveyance—broadcaster, if you will—of information about the library, including what new materials have been acquired. These announcements of "new arrivals" take the form of not simple listings of titles but of short-length—though authoritative and helpful—reviews. Generally, these reviews are written by library staff members.

In addition to websites, reviews of new library books and audiobooks are also useful in the preparation of readers' advisory handouts: pamphlets, brochures, bookmarks, or single sheets that can be placed in the hands of library patrons to connect a title they have just read or to which they have listened to another item the librarian guesses—an *educated* guess, that is—will also appeal to that particular patron.

These reviews appearing in readers' advisory handouts can be the same reviews prepared by library staff members for the library website. After all, these reviews, once prepared, are library "property" and then can be used in any fashion library personnel deem necessary or advisable in the promotion of library services to the general public. One size fits all: in this case, one review fits all.

If your library has a blog written or administered by a staff person, what better place to broadcast your new arrivals? Here, too, a simple listing of new titles will not suffice. A rundown of new arrivals on a blog would also necessitate review writing, obviously by the blogmaster or other staff members. But the difference in a blog discussion of new arrivals would be just that: a *discussion*. The blogmaster should present the reviews written by staff members for the website but also stretch them out into more of an "oral report." The blog reader is served by the reviews and by the conversational approach to book news:

> "Here's what the author of this book says about this topic."
>
> "In the news yesterday was a story about such and such, and this new book ties in with the essence of that story."
>
> "I was reminded the other day of what a strong effect our pets have on our lives, and that theme is a major thread in this new novel we have recently added to our fiction collection."

BOOK CLUBS

Book clubs remain popular, the majority of them set within the context of the private home, where friends and acquaintances gather to discuss and even argue over a previously agreed-upon book.

Library-sponsored book clubs also remain big business; and, of course, book-club members discovering new titles to read and share thoughts about is an ongoing concern. To support book clubs can mean that public libraries not only make space available but also make themselves a resource for book-club reading suggestions, which, of course, means supplying interested book-club members with reviews of new arrivals: reviews that have been prepared by staff members for original use on the library website.

BEYOND THE WALLS OF THE LIBRARY

Last, but not particularly least, many librarians may have an interest in learning how to write reviews with the aim of pursuing their own freelance-writing careers. Librarians interested in freelance reviewing will customarily focus their pursuit of acquiring reviewing assignments from newspapers, general-circulation magazines, or professional journals.

Most anything a librarian does in the direction of freelance reviewing will reflect positively on the institution for which the librarian works. Author identification accompanying the byline generally will indicate the author's library position. This is, of course, good library public relations and marketing.

Short reviews for the library website, long reviews for a newspaper: how to write either kind is not necessarily instinctive. Help is usually needed. This book you now have in your hands offers such instruction, moving now to a discussion of the differences between reviewing and writing criticism.

REVIEWS VERSUS CRITICISM 2

Whether one writes reviews or chooses to focus on criticism instead (and the two differ greatly), it all boils down to opin-ion; and, of course, what one person's opinion happens to be is certainly not what someone else's opinion will be. Let's start off with the subjectivity of reviewing.

When I was a librarian at Cleveland Public Library, the head of the library's public relations department gave a staff-training presentation during one of those close-the-doors-to-the-public staff-education days. One of the points she emphasized was subjectivity. She read a short sentence giving a positive slant to a well-known book and then one giving a negative slant to the same book.

I want to borrow the exercise from her, using *Gone with the Wind* (*GWTW*), because everyone knows the basic story line and the main character. *GWTW* could be summarized in this way:

> The drama of the Civil War and Reconstruction is rendered powerfully and movingly as a backdrop to following the adventures of a gutsy woman, Scarlett O'Hara, in trying to remake a life for herself in a world torn asunder.

But now this:

> Who could care whether this Scarlett O'Hara person will ever go hungry again? She's petty, her story is petty, and Margaret Mitchell has trivialized the whole Civil War period by focusing on such a nonheroic character as Scarlett.

Each stance, positive and negative, is a valid assessment of the famous novel, depending on how the novel—or, more specifically, the main character—struck the reader. It's all about opinion: a well-considered, well-informed opinion but an *opinion* nevertheless.

SOME PROCEDURES AND RULES

Regardless of the subjective nature of reviewing, we can nevertheless isolate some procedures and rules that will help us compose effective reviews and in the process learn how to judge the quality of reviews we encounter every day and in the course of our work.

We begin by making an important distinction: *reviewing* is different from *criticism*. Despite the popular perception that the two terms are synonymous and the two practices are the same, they are not: reviewing is one thing, and criticism is another.

A WALK UP BELLOSGUARDO HILL: REVIEWING

To illustrate the difference, accompany me now on two journeys. In the first, I share an entry from my journal that recalls a particular trip I took to Italy:

> A bright, warm, but not overly hot day dawned—again. So far our time in Florence has been blessed with the perfect weather that made us only too pleased to hear from other guests in the hotel that we should be glad we weren't in the city last week, when torrents of rain fell in a several-day stretch.
>
> The place where we were now headed—fortified with our food supplies—would be very new to us. Off we went, across the south bank of the Arno and to the southwestern verge of the city proper, where the urban look and feel quickly gave way to Tuscan countryside, from flat ground to hilly.
>
> Ah, the famous Florentine hills! With map in hand and no trepidation, we marched up the Via Bellosguardo, scaling the soft flank of the particular Florentine hill after which the road was named.
>
> The Via Bellosguardo combined a sense of suburban street and rural road, paved but nevertheless narrow and hemmed in on one side by a tall, thick stone wall, which was topped by shards of glass, at first

glance looking like sugar crystals garnishing a pastry, obviously to keep people from climbing over. On the other side of the via, the far side of the container wall, the sides of villas came flush up against the roadbed. But periodic open spaces between the villas afforded us delicious peeks at gardens and olive groves.

The beauty of Florence only increased as we pulled back to see it in its entirety, nestled in its valley by the Arno. It's like stepping back from a large painting to see the cumulative effect of its details rather than simply seeing only the details, rich and precise though they may be.

Once back down into the city proper, sitting in my favorite Florentine café, I opened my journal and recorded, in as much colorful and resonant detail as I could, my impressions of our hike.

What you have read is a *review*—first impressions of the lay of the land. In my complete entry for that particular episode, I recalled the beautiful play of color over the shanks of the distant hills across the valley in which Florence nestles; wild blossoms poking their colorful faces through a crack in the wall running alongside the road up the hill; a villa whose front door we faced as we sat for a moment before our descent back into the city center, the villa itself an arrangement of beige pink boxes. I concluded with a qualitative judgment of the whole experience: Had we been wise in choosing that particular path up into the Florentine hills? Was the famous view, mentioned in every guidebook, as sublime as expected? Did it pan out for us, or were we disappointed, and if so, why?

THE NORMAN CONQUEST UNDER ENGLAND'S HENRY II: CRITICISM

Now permit me to digress once again, with another travel anecdote relevant to our discussion. It took place several years prior to my Florentine experience, on my first visit to Europe, between my junior and senior years in college. I attended a summer-study-abroad program, at Trinity College in Dublin, Ireland. The purpose of the program was to live among Irish college students and research a topic, then write a paper on it for college credit. The libraries at Trinity College were thrown open to us, as was the main library at University College; but the chief thrill was access to the beautiful reading room of the National Library of Ireland and, concomitantly, permission to use that library's materials and resources.

We always did our duty and spent several hours with our noses in books at one or another of the libraries open to us, but we also made time to explore every neighborhood of that ancient, richly atmospheric city.

My research topic was the Norman Conquest of Ireland: specifically, the preliminary stages of this monumental wave that swept over the island, instigated and directed by King Henry II of England, who initiated a process of bringing French-Norman culture into Ireland. In pursuit of my topic, I had an opportunity to examine in the National Library a priceless, old book about the Norman Conquest that had been published during the reign of Queen Elizabeth I. (The library clerk on duty said, perhaps in jest but perhaps not, that probably no one had actually handled the book *since* the reign of the first Elizabeth.) I also traveled to the seaside town of Wicklow and stood on the beach where, eight hundred years before, Henry II and his longbowmen made landfall.

In this case, I was not engaged in "reviewing" Ireland as I would "review" Florence a few years later, looking at the city and gathering relatively general impressions for my journal. Instead, in Ireland, I had set out to analyze in depth one particular facet of Irish civilization: one special aspect of Irish history, the Norman Conquest under England's Henry II.

DIFFERENCE BETWEEN REVIEWING AND CRITICISM

This is the fundamental difference between reviewing and criticism: reviewing is broader, more encompassing, and less specific than criticism. A review is a survey, a sharing of first impressions, an appraisal of all aspects in relative balance. Criticism has a specific focus, a concentration on one and usually only one quality, feature, characteristic, or strain appearing in or running through, for example, the narrative of a book or movie or audiobook.

Up to this point, I have been discussing reviewing versus criticism in general terms, drawing parallels between journal writing about Florence and the practice of reviewing, and between in-depth coverage of one aspect of Irish history and literary criticism. Now I'll move from generalities to the differences between reviewing and criticism in terms specific to library materials.

Reviewing represents an assessment of something new "on the market": something just recently released or about to be released. Criticism can be thought of as a considered, sharply focused look at a book or nonprint item that was new *a few years ago*, or, more often than not, *several years ago*. Timeliness—talking about something new that other people are going to be talking about—is not an issue in criticism.

Reviews function as announcements of new materials. They are really news items that appear either before or more or less immediately after the release of a book, with the addition of a reviewer's editorializing: here's a glimpse of a brand new book I just read, and here's what I have to say about it.

AUDIENCE

One more very big difference between reviewing and criticism needs to be spelled out: *audience*. Although overlap certainly occurs, the audience for reviewing differs from the audience for criticism.

Criticism is aimed at scholars or at least very serious readers interested in being taken well inside a topic or a piece of creative writing, way beyond an appraisal of the "lay of the land." Most reviews are written for general readers looking for a good book (and for librarians involved in collection development). Of course, scholars read reviews, too, but they turn to criticism to satisfy their need for deeper understanding.

AN EXAMPLE OF LITERARY CRITICISM

It would be instructive to look at a specific example of literary criticism. In spring 2001, the estimable literary magazine *Southern Review* published a piece titled "Possessions in *The Great Gatsby*," written by Scott Donaldson, a professor emeritus of English at the College of William and Mary and author of well-received biographies of writers F. Scott Fitzgerald and John Cheever.

Donaldson takes quite an in-depth probe into F. Scott Fitzgerald's masterpiece, and his essay stands, in perfect opposition for our purposes, as literary criticism in contrast to reviewing. In twenty-three pages, Donaldson, utilizing the fullness that such a number of pages accords him, investigates the "appurtenances" (accessories) that mark the social status and aspirations of the characters in *Gatsby*.[1] He surmises and concludes that one of the lessons of the novel is that one cannot escape self-definition as revealed by one's accessories: "one's house, one's clothes: they do express one's self."[2] Specifically, Gatsby's "clothes, his car, his house, his parties—all brand him as newly rich."[3]

Donaldson identifies the possessions and personality traits of other characters in the novel as well, all of which affix, despite the characters' lack of intention in that regard, certain labels onto their roots and intentions in life. For instance, Myrtle Wilson, Tom Buchanan's mistress, exposes her lower-class origins by buying cold cream and perfume from a drugstore cosmetics counter, by letting several empty cabs pass her by until one in a loud color comes by, by dissing her help, by feigning indifference toward a dress she obviously chose for its showiness, and by displaying unconventional grammar. Donaldson sees that for the characters—including Gatsby himself—ascending to the upper class is not just about obtaining money. As they desire to rise above their original station, the one into which they were born, his characters obtain possessions that are the *very* possessions to truly connote wealth and cultivation.

This essay is rather erudite, sophisticated commentary. By no means is it a lay-of-the-land overview of the plot and characters in *Gatsby*, but it is, rather, a teasing out of one particular thread running through the story, a vital and certainly resonant fabric of this great American novel. Three important questions must be considered: Would you read the essay before actually reading the novel itself? Would the essay be instructive without having read *Gatsby* beforehand? Would reading the essay without having read the novel *compel* you to read it? Perhaps one might answer yes to the last of the three questions, but could the answer to the first two questions be anything other than no?

Criticism makes far less sense to someone who has not read the text that is being analyzed. The parameters of the picture as presented in a piece of criticism simply do not reveal the full extent of the frame and thus do not give a full idea of what a book is about. But reviews are a completely different story.

BREAKING DOWN A BOOK REVIEW

Although the critical essay is not intended to provide a full idea of what a book is about, a review should indeed demarcate the fullest boundaries of a book or nonprint item.

Let's break down an example. In the February 25, 2001, edition of the *New York Times Book Review*, widely applauded short-story writer Rick Moody's collection *Demonology* was reviewed by Walter Kirn, former literary editor of *GQ* magazine and a fiction writer in his own right. Kirn begins his review with a wise, provocative maxim: "Good short-story collections, like good record albums, are almost always hit-and-miss affairs—successful if they include three or four great tracks, wildly successful if they have five."[4]

His reviewing wisdom and generosity, to say nothing of his beautifully atmospheric writing style, is well exercised as he proceeds to develop the metaphor of story collection as record album:

> A story collection that's uniformly appealing is just as suspect, and probably as unimaginative, as an album composed of nothing but catchy singles. Short stories are fiction's R&B department, and failed or less than conclusive experiments are not just to be expected but to be hoped for. Let the novelists fret about consistency—story writers should feel free to jam; to get things right in new, surprising ways by allowing themselves, now and then, to get things wrong.[5]

The introductory comments in Kirn's creatively metaphoric and securely knowledgeable review set the wide parameters of not only the book under review but also the boundaries of his review to come. He hasn't staked out just a little patch of the book and consequently plans to send down a drill for a core sampling as if he were exploring for oil, but instead he's spread the whole book out and indicates the path by which he will explore the whole lay of the land as it has unfolded before him.

Kirn continues the music metaphor in his second paragraph, bringing his opening axiom down to specific application in Moody's *Demonology*. "Between its displays of sure accomplishment—its gratifying half-dozen or so hits—it flies off on tangents. . . . If Moody were in a rock band, he'd be the drummer, with a flair for wild, showy solos that occasionally go on too long or indulge in fancy feats of skill impressive only to other drummers but that can also, when they find their own logic and their groove, awe and energize."[6]

So, do you see what Kirn is doing in the opening two paragraphs of his review? He is accomplishing what a good reviewer should accomplish: quickly establishing the full scope of the book and identifying its boundaries.

Kirn explores some individual stories, turning then over and around to observe them at their best angle but also, as we have expected from his opening two paragraphs, to see if flaws in structure are present or, if Moody were a gem cutter, in the way he took a solid piece of crystal and cut facets in less-than-advantageous angles. But then Kirn comes around again to drawing conclusions about the book as a whole, and also back on the same metaphoric track he'd set down for himself in his first paragraph: "Every good laboratory has some broken test tubes, and every hit has a flip side. Enjoy the hits."[7]

When reading and analyzing this well-conceived review, three ideas should be kept in mind:

Idea one is that the musical metaphor that Kirn so imaginatively employs is a particularly effective *framing device* for the review, by which the reader is looking, as happens in all reviews so defined as "reviews," at the book as a whole, in all its qualities, characteristics, and effectiveness or lack thereof. A framing device, such as Kirn's, is almost necessary to keep a long review from sprawling, from losing its focus, and thus from losing the reader's attention and interest.

Idea two builds on the previous point. If this review were not a review but a piece of literary criticism, it would run longer than even a long review; furthermore, Kirn would have isolated *actual* musical metaphors within each story and disregarded all other aspects of the stories.

Idea three is that criticism is generally longer, yes, but it is not so easy to determine if what you have before you is a piece of criticism or a review *just* by its length. That is why it is essential to keep in mind the basic definitions of criticism and reviewing.

THE QUESTION OF LENGTH

There you have it: a review offers the reader a general statement about the wide scope of the item under review, a general mapping out of the whole area.

But a reviewer's requirement to survey the whole "country" a book covers does not necessarily mean that a review has to be a required length—a substantial length—to successfully accomplish that task. To put it another way, no matter how brief a review, even a capsule review, it is absolutely necessary for it to establish the full boundaries of a book's scope. That may be all the room the review has: to describe the "map" of the book. There must be some accompanying critical commentary, too, for it to qualify as a review as opposed to a simple, nonanalytic annotation. (*Annotation* is defined, in concrete and specific terms, in appendix A. Suffice it to say now, an annotation is a twenty-five- to fifty-word description of a book or audiobook.)

The reviews offered in the "Briefly Noted" section of the *New Yorker* are splendid examples of the effectiveness of a review under 150 words; they are perfect showcases for how a short review can, with sheer eloquence, impart the lay of a book's land: in a few brief brushstrokes let the reader know the territory this particular book stakes out.

The following review, from the "Briefly Noted" section, exemplifies how a review that is short can be both short *and* complete.

Marie Antoinette: The Journey, by Antonia Fraser
(Doubleday; $35).

Reliable and absorbing as ever, Fraser's blend of insight and research persuades us that this unfortunate queen deserves neither the vilification nor the idealization she has received. Marie Antoinette was merely a pretty, sketchily educated teenager when, in 1770, she was shipped from Vienna to Versailles as the bride of the heir to the French throne, in a deal arranged by her mother, Empress Maria Teresa, and the French King Louis XV. She lived in a court preoccupied by petty feuds, where few people noticed the decay of the ancien régime and those who did disagreed about remedies. Fraser argues that the Queen was a scapegoat, accused of being, at once, a frivolous, featherbrained hedonist and a dangerous, Machiavellian plotter. While her rule was not exemplary, her execution, in 1793, was hardly a victory for popular government.[8]

This is an excellent example of a short review *not* requiring a framing device. While giving the reader a broad picture of the book's field of inquiry, it does not sprawl, it does not spill over the sides, and it does not lose reader interest.

The reader of the review knows exactly the area staked out by the book at hand: simply and directly, the life of the ill-fated queen of France. In short space, this review has successfully surveyed the lay of the land. Not probed it in depth, not isolated one small part of Fraser's book to analyze in concentration, not carried on an exercise of criticism. This is a review, a short but effectively—even beautifully—written review. Distinct from criticism, obviously.

NOTES

1. Scott Donaldson, "Possessions in *The Great Gatsby*," criticism of *The Great Gatsby*, by F. Scott Fitzgerald, *Southern Review* 37 (spring 2001): 188.

2. Ibid.

3. Ibid.

4. Walter Kirn, "Lexical Overdrive," review of *Demonology*, by Rick Moody, *New York Times Book Review* (February 25, 2001): 12.

5. Ibid.

6. Ibid.

7. Ibid., 13.

8. "*Marie Antoinette: The Journey*, by Antonia Fraser," "Briefly Noted," *New Yorker* (September 24, 2001): 93. Copyright 2001 Conde Nast Publication. All rights reserved. Originally published in the *New Yorker* (September 24, 2001). Reprinted by permission.

TWO KINDS OF REVIEWS: 3
BEFORE PUBLICATION AND
AFTER PUBLICATION

GALLEY PROOFS, OR ADVANCE
READING COPIES

The path a book takes to the point of publication, beginning with the signing of a contract between publisher and writer, usually includes a galley-proof stage. In the "old days," when I first entered the publishing industry, some thirty years ago, galley proofs were exactly what the term implies: a preliminary printing of the manuscript for a proofreader to make one last pass through, at this point hopefully not making substantive changes but just cosmetic ones: correcting hard-to-detect, previously unnoticed typos or making minor corrections in formatting. These galley proofs were not fancily bound, more often not bound at all, but simply folded sheets. If they *were* bound, the binding was simple and temporary, the pages often falling loose in the hand by the time someone got halfway through reading it. The covers were simply thick-stock paper, undecorated, with the author's name, the title of the book, the publisher, and other relevant publishing information (price, month and year of publication, ISBN) printed in plain type across the otherwise drab face.

These days, however, a galley proof is often referred to as an "advance reading copy" (ARC) by the publisher; and that is, indeed, the primary function of this stage in the path a book takes to getting published. Anymore, the editing and proofreading are done by galley-proof stage, and the real purpose of producing bound galleys is for submission to the prepublication review media, for reviewers' evaluation before its publication date. (ARCs are also made available to readers' advisory librarians as a promotional step in creating interest and buzz.)

Thus, no expense is spared in the production of galley proofs these days. The text is in its final format; the design of the pages is as it will appear in the final, finished product. The binding is tight, pages reluctant to tear loose as before. The covers are colorful and even flashy—most often, the front cover is a facsimile of the dust jacket that will adorn the finished book when it appears.

In all, galley proofs are as substantial and attractive as paperback versions, and in many instances it is difficult to tell if what you have in your hands is a galley proof or a paperback edition of the finished book—and all to catch the notice of the prepublication review media.

PREPUBLICATION REVIEW MEDIA

Not just librarians count on the prepublication reviews. Booksellers must always be aware of what is going to be published in the near future, so orders can be placed right away; and the place to which most booksell-

---

HOOPER'S REVIEWS

Innocent Traitor,
by Alison Weir (Ballantine, 2007)

The title of this complex yet completely absorbing novel reflects the author's point of view as she reconstructs the life of the unfortunate Lady Jane Grey. That this is popular historian Weir's first novel is publishing news. Lady Jane Grey was a great-niece of King Henry VIII of England, and the term *political pawn* could have been invented for her. In alternating voices, each distinctively authentic, Weir lets Lady Jane and other individuals involved in her life and fate tell their sides of the story, and what a story it is. King Henry, it will be remembered, had succession problems: namely, until his marriage to his third wife, he had no male heir. Added to that was the age's seemingly irresolvable conflict between Protestants and Catholics. Therein lay the trouble for the teenage Lady Jane. She was thrust by her power-hungry and caustically Protestant parents into a plot to place her on the throne upon the death of the little king Edward VI, the late king Henry's Protestant son, instead of the legal heiress, the Catholic princess Mary. Mary won the day and throne, and Lady Jane went to the block. Weir finds Jane an intelligent individual, a thinker in her own right; but, tragically, given the times and the power available to the "grown-ups" around her, she ultimately could not resist the political currents swirling over her. A brilliantly vivid and psychologically astute novel.

Booklist, November 15, 2006

ers turn for advance notice of soon-to-be-published books is the magazine *Publishers Weekly*, whose pages carry trade news, interviews, and reviews of upcoming books, which are pretty much the length of the "Briefly Noted" reviews in the *New Yorker*. There are also catalogs and brochures and other promotional materials sent out by publishers, social and gossip columns in newspapers, blogs, and entertainment programs on television (where celebrities' intentions to soon be writing a book are often announced), but the prepublication journals—which also include *Booklist* and *Library Journal*—form an essential, dependable, and often entertaining source.

Just as the book buyers for national chains have to be aware of the imminent publication of major books, so, too, must librarians make certain that when important books are published, and reviews of them begin appearing in the national news media, these books be on their library shelves as soon as possible. For that to happen, librarians consult the prepublication review media.

The prepublication review magazines *Booklist, Publishers Weekly,* and *Library Journal* publish reviews geared toward librarians selecting new titles for purchase. In addition, reviews in *Booklist* and *Library Journal* often indicate comparisons between the book or nonprint title under review and other works or writers or narrators of a similar nature or style, to help librarians in readers' advisory.

As a result, whether readers choose to buy a book or borrow a book, they can depend on booksellers and librarians to provide what they want (and generally when they want it, too). Just ask Mister X (see "To Buy or Borrow: That Is the Question").

Thus, there are two kinds of reviews: one, those appearing in *advance* of a book or audiobook's release, for the arming of booksellers and librarians with important information on forthcoming items needing to be considered for purchase in order to please, in the first circumstance, bookstore customers, and in the second circumstance, public library borrowers. The other type of reviews are those appearing at the time of a book or audiobook's release date (or even after), the purpose of which is to inform the reading public of new book or nonprint items that are out and ready for public consumption, either by securing in a bookstore or in the local library. Reviews also appear in scholarly or professional journals to make scholars and professionals aware of newly released titles perhaps requiring their professional attention.

TO BUY OR BORROW: THAT IS THE QUESTION

It is Sunday morning. Mister X, a well-read man in early middle age, sits in his living room with a second cup of coffee at hand, relaxing and reading the Sunday *New York Times*. He reads the first section first, to be made aware of the most important news events of the day, and because he enjoys traveling, he picks up the travel section next, making a mental note to clip out the short piece on hotels in Buenos Aires, a destination he has placed at the top of his "desire" list.

Being well read, Mister X now turns to the estimable, influential *New York Times Book Review*. Within its reliably well-written pages, Mister X's interest is soon riveted by a review of a book on presidential history by a man often appearing on the evening news-discussion shows on television. Mister X decides he really has no other choice but to read the book; he simply has too much interest in the subject and the author not to read it, and the reviewer has indicated in no uncertain terms how excellent is the book's coverage. So, the decision to read it was really no decision at all for Mister X. But now he does face a real decision, which, before he can get his hands on the book and enjoy its informative pages, he must come to terms with. The issue he now faces is this: Go to a bookstore and purchase the book, or go to the pubic library and borrow a copy for the short term?

The decision is Mister X's to make. But here on Sunday morning he is determined to have the book in hand by Monday noon. His personal motivations—whether he decides to buy the book rather than borrow it from his local public library—are really not our concern. What is our concern is what Mister X expects to happen, with passages of the glowing review still in mind as he weighs the decision to buy or borrow a copy.

Either way, he expects to find the book on the shelves: on the bookstore shelves if he has decided to purchase it, or on the library shelves if he has made the decision to borrow a copy. The *New York Times Book Review* has announced to him that this wonderful new book is out, and he expects it to be out, to be available to him.

Buy

Let us say that Mister X decides to purchase the book. On Monday morning during his lunch hour, he steps out of his office and walks down, say, Michigan Avenue in Chicago, to the big Border's Bookstore located up the avenue a few blocks from his office. He enters the revolving door, disregards the information desk, for he is pretty certain he will find what he is looking for by himself. Sure enough, from a few feet away from the "New Arrivals

Nonfiction" display table, he spots the book in which he's interested. Flipping through the pages only confirms his decision to not only read it but also to own it, and in a matter of only a few minutes, he's back out the bookstore door, a successful sale on the part of Border's having just taken place, easily and comfortably for both parties involved: bookseller and new book owner.

But something had to happen before this successful transaction—successful for Mister X as well as for the bookseller—could unfold in quick effectiveness. The bookseller had to be aware of the recent publication of the book (which, as it turns out, Mr. X wanted) to have his orders made in time so that when the book rolled off the printing line, he would have copies in his store waiting for people like Mister X, who, when reading the reviews coming out at the time of the book's publication, would then come in to buy a copy.

Borrow

Let us say—for the sake of argument—that Mister X did not actually need to own the interesting book of which he read the review in the *New York Times Book Review* but simply borrow it to read. So, on his Monday lunch break, Mister X hops on a bus heading south on Michigan Avenue, and in a few minutes, he jumps off for a two-block walk to the Harold Washington Library, the main library in the vast Chicago Public Library system. Familiar with the computerized card catalog, Mister X flips through a few screens and learns that the library not only possesses the book he wants to read but still has a copy remaining on the shelf. A brief consultation with the floor chart reminds him what floor to head to and where on that floor the appropriate section should be found.

Voilà, the desired book, its dust jacket covered in new plastic protection, and Mister X thinks of slipcovers on furniture as he takes the book back down to the circulation desk for checking out.

Mister X walks out of the library pleased with the smoothness of the operation he has just experienced. He desired to read the book, and he secured it; he wanted no trouble or delay in obtaining it, and he was met with no trouble or delay. But unbeknownst to him—but *important* to him, in fact—events and procedures had to fall into place within the offices of the library prior to Mister X's visit there to ensure his visit's productive outcome. The librarians at Harold Washington Library had to make certain that when this important book got published and reviews of it began appearing in the national news media, it would be on their library shelves, and it was. And thus did Mister X get his book.

DIFFERING PHILOSOPHIES

Now, we have divided the universe of reviewing into a bipartite realm: reviews that appear in advance of a book's publication or nonprint material's release and those making their appearance upon or after a book's publication or nonprint title's release.

Differing philosophies operate behind these two halves of the review world. Reviews appearing in the popular press—such as the *New York Times Book Review, Time, Newsweek,* and *Gentleman's Quarterly,* to name only a few examples—and those appearing usually quite a bit after the item's publication in scholarly or professional journals—such as *Georgia Review* or *Public Libraries*—are addressed to people who are potential readers of the book being reviewed.

Reviews appearing in the prepublication review media—*Booklist, Publishers Weekly,* and *Library Journal*—are addressed, on the other hand, not to readers who are necessarily going to read the book or listen to the audiobook but who will be purchasing it either for their bookstore or their library.

So, what do those differences mean in terms of the information the review contains? For one thing, prepublication reviews often note how a librarian can use this particular book in a library collection: for instance, its potential reference value in answering a library patron's questions about a certain subject; its value in contributing to a comprehensive collection of, say, books on the Civil War; or its appeal or nonappeal to readers of only serious literature. Additionally, comments might be made as to how booksellers or public librarians should stock up on books bound to be very popular and on the various best-seller lists.

The reviewer might also make readers' advisory suggestions to the librarian. Readers' advisory is a function that librarians usually enjoy most of all their duties and responsibilities, because it involves being relied on by library patrons for help in finding just the kind of book they love to read, based on their personal subject interests and fiction tastes as well as other writers they have enjoyed. Take, for instance, this concluding statement in a *Booklist* review of a novel titled *The Destruction of the Inn,* by Randy Lee Eickhoff: "Readers interested in mythology and Irish folklore will thrill to this fast-paced epic, which should please both scholar and layperson alike."[1] You can readily see that this is not a comment addressed to someone who is deciding whether to read the book but to a librarian deciding upon its purchase.

HOW LIBRARIANS SELECT BOOKS

It might be instructive at this point to provide an overview of the basic tenets of selection in libraries—those taught in master's programs in library science and thus second nature to practicing librarians.

A librarian studies the prepublication review media and, as backup, peruses reviews in the popular press. These after-publication reviews are used to make certain that books and audiobooks that should have been ordered for one's particular collection and community have not been overlooked; moreover, by scanning reviews in the popular press, librarians might reconsider purchasing a title that they did not originally deem necessary for inclusion in their collection.

When librarians—whether public, school, or academic—examine either of these two types of reviews, two factors must be considered in

HOOPER'S REVIEWS

Fado, by Andrzej Stasiuk,
tr. by Bill Johnston (Dalkey Archive, 2009)

The author is an award-winning Polish writer, and his new book is a compilation of travel essays that constitutes the latest volume in the publisher's Polish Literature series, bringing to U.S. readers otherwise unobtainable English-language translations of important writings in that language. Resting on the sentiment that "to travel is to live. Or in any case to live doubly, triply, multiple times," Stasiuk's style of travel writing takes readers, in beautifully descriptive prose, to far and often remote corners of Eastern Europe. He is an alluring writer; the opening line of "Highway," the first essay in the collection—"Best of all is night in a foreign country"—is a siren song guaranteeing the book will not be put down until the last page has been read. His sense of Romania—"past, present, and future coexist there, and decay walks arm in arm with growth"—serves as an overriding metaphor for every place to which he wanders in Eastern Europe. No chamber of commerce boosterism here; instead, he offers the truth, often harsh, as he sees it as he explores places for the most part unexplored by even the most experienced American traveler.

Booklist, July 2009

their decision to purchase a particular book or nonprint item. First, are these books or audiobooks of currently high but soon-to-wear-off interest to the public (such as titles on the O. J. Simpson trial a few years ago)? Books and audiobooks on very topical subjects must be ordered quickly and gotten into the collection immediately, and perhaps even more than a single copy should be acquired. After the general public's interest in this particular person or event has slackened, these books and audiobooks are often candidates for weeding; on the other hand, if some of the books on that now-desiccated issue are good, solid treatments, they may remain permanently in the collection.

Second, a librarian must always be conscious of collecting books and audiobooks that are not about hot topics but are of more lasting value to the serviceability of the library collection as a whole. These titles would include, for instance, manuals on home repair, a new and necessary biography of First Lady Florence Harding, the latest novel by a very serious writer who has a devoted but not wide readership, and the first book to collect all the poetry of an estimable American poet.

There are two kinds of reviews: prepublication reviews used by librarians and booksellers to get the jump on what readers are going to be asking for, and upon-publication or after-publication reviews in the popular media, for readers to see if they want to read a particular book or listen to a particular audiobook.

Both kinds of reviews are used by librarians in material selection: for the permanent collection; for the "popular" collection, reflecting immediate and probably impermanent library-patron interest; and, of course, for readers' advisory needs in the library.

NOTE

1. Brendan Dowling, review of *The Destruction of the Inn*, by Randy Lee Eickhoff, *Booklist* 97 (March 15, 2001): 1353.

WHAT IS IN A BOOK REVIEW? 4

A HARD-AND-FAST RULE

Every book review, whether long or short—500 words or 175 words in length—is required to tell the reader of the review two important things: What is the book about? How good is it?

This is a hard-and-fast rule of book reviewing. (In chapter 8, Joyce Saricks covers audiobook reviewing, showing the differences between it and book reviewing.) A successful review *must* answer the question of what the book is about and the question of how well it is done. A review deserving of the name "review" *must* answer, in varying depth (depending on the length of the review) those two questions, so the reader of the review will have what then amounts to a "profile" of the book, which is exactly what a review is supposed to provide.

Both kinds of reviews—prepublication reviews so vital to librarians and booksellers, and after-publication reviews appearing in the pages of the popular media relied upon by the general reading public for their personal enjoyment and edification—require that both of these two questions be answered. When a reviewer has a book in hand, whether fiction or nonfiction, the reviewer's consciousness during the reading process must be focused on how these two questions will be answered when the time comes to put pen to paper (or fingertips to keyboard).

HOW MUCH SPACE FOR EACH QUESTION

The proportional space in the review devoted to answering each of the two questions will vary according to the emphasis the reviewer deems most important to the reader: Is telling the reader what the book is about the most important concern, or is evaluating the book's success or failure what the reader should know more about?

Chances are, the reviewer will give more space to the first question than the second; most reviewers, you will find, emphasize a book's content over its quality.

That represents not a rule for reviewing but simply one of its most salient traits: information on what the book under review is about is of primary importance and interest either to a librarian curious about the book's potential place in his or her library collection or to the potential general-interest reader of the book perusing, say, the *New York Times Book Review* on a Sunday morning. The book's success or failure in achieving its purpose is not necessarily of secondary weight, but it makes better sense to learn first what the book is about. And, somewhat ironically, how well the book performs its task is usually easier to express in a more compact fashion than giving the reader a picture of a book's contents; the former *can* be accomplished in a handful of words, but the latter needs more time and space to be articulated.

MORE SPACE ALLOTTED TO CONTENT

More time is usually given to what a book is about than how good it is. This applies to brief reviews as well as much longer reviews running to several pages. Take, for example, a recent review in *Booklist*, the prepublication review journal published by the American Library Association in Chicago, the magazine for which I work. The book under review is called *Comfort Me with Apples: More Adventures at the Table*, written by Ruth Reichl, published by Random in April 2001, and reviewed by Mark Knoblauch.[1]

The opening line of this short review reads: "The second volume of noted gourmet Reichl's memoirs finds her as an aspiring novelist who, to make ends meet, has just accepted a position as restaurant critic for a California magazine."

How well Knoblauch has easily, quickly, and comfortably opened the door for the reader onto what type of book is under consideration here. In very few words, amounting to sheer and eloquent language, the reviewer identifies the author and her professional credentials and throws first light on the book's general aim.

In his next rich but not overwrought sentence, Knoblauch opens the door further to broaden our understanding of where the book takes the reader: "Married to a successful artist and living in a Berkeley commune, Reichl embarks on her new career under the tutelage of food writer Colman Andrews, who whisks her off to Paris and schools her in arts both gustatory and amatory."

The reviewer goes on to trace the course of the rest of the book, which follows the course of events in the author's life up to the point at which she intends to leave the story, apparently to be continued in a subsequent volume of memoir. These major events that are covered in the book are mentioned in the review, and they include the end of her affair, the continuation of her involvement in the world of California cuisine, and, eventually, the securing of an important restaurant-critic position. Her concurrent personal life is centered on a new marriage and starting a family.

There we have it. Two lines of this concise yet very expressive review have been given over to answering the question, What is the book about? Now the reviewer proceeds to offer an answer to the second essential question, How good is it?

HOOPER'S REVIEWS

Cleaving: A Story of Marriage, Meat, and Obsession, by Julie Powell (Little, Brown, 2009)

The author of the charming, riveting, thrilling—and successfully filmed—*Julie and Julia* (2005), in which Powell recounted her year spent cooking all the recipes in Julia Child's classic *Mastering the Art of French Cooking*, has turned to butchery! As she relays in her new memoir, after her "year with Julia," she apprenticed in a butcher shop in upstate New York and learned the trade from the inside out, from sinew to steak. Another prominent theme here is the stress placed on her marriage to the understanding, even noble Eric (as he was depicted in the previous memoir) by their mutual infidelities. It's a grim book. Powell's fans happily voyaged with her through Julia Child's cookbook, but taking the journey through her learning the "art" of butchery is another matter. Graphic, even gross, detail about "breaking down" a beef or pig carcass and about her adulterous sex life (Do we really want to hear about her phone sex with her lover?) blocks any sunshine from emerging from these pages. The previous book made "foodies" of us all, but this book may convince us that vegetarians have had the right idea all along.

Booklist, December 15, 2009

We read such comments as "her tragic tale, touchingly rendered," and "those who reveled in Reichl's portrait of her mother in *Tender at the Bone* (1998) will find even more delightful characters in this new volume." The reviewer ends with a last piece of information about the book, making in direct fashion a concluding note of critical evaluation.

But rather than simply quoting the last line by itself, let us place it in context by quoting the entire review; this, after all, will be the best instruction—now that we have taken the review apart to isolate the information on content, the evaluative evidence, and the tidy last line— on how all the parts work so successfully in ensemble.

> The second volume of noted gourmet Reichl's memoirs finds her as an aspiring novelist who, to make ends meet, has just accepted a position as restaurant critic for a California magazine. Married to a successful artist and living in a Berkeley commune, Reichl embarks on her new career under the tutelage of food writer Colman Andrews, who whisks her off to Paris and schools her in arts both gustatory and amatory. Although the affair ends when Andrews marries another woman, Reichl profited from her lover's broad knowledge and his insider's view of the food world. Soon she is caught up in the emergence of California cuisine and joins that influential circle that encompasses Alice Waters, Jonathan Waxman, and Wolfgang Puck. Eventually offered the restaurant critic's seat at the *Los Angeles Times,* Reichl moves to Southern California and into a new marriage. Lest one believe that the restaurant critic's job offers no serious challenges, Reichl recounts an early incident in which her lack of journalistic experience jeopardized her new position and nearly cost her her job. Determined to start a family, she consults fertility specialists and eventually decides on adoption. Her tragic tale, touchingly rendered, about her struggle to adopt a daughter ends with Reichl and her extraordinarily supportive husband bitterly disappointed; however, they are soon full of new hope when she discovers that she's pregnant. Those who reveled in Reichl's portrait of her mother in *Tender at the Bone* (1998) will find even more delightful characters in this new volume. Recipes scattered throughout the text mark off periods in the author's growth.[2]

A LONG REVIEW'S ANSWERS
TO THE DUAL QUESTIONS

Now let us look at how a reviewer in a long review handles the necessary answering of the two important questions any review must answer—and, more specifically, the percentage of the review given over to each answer. A wonderfully illustrative example—and beautifully written as well—can be found in novelist Francine Prose's review of *The Complete Works of Isaac Babel* (Norton) in *Harper's*, November 2001. This is a stunningly wrought review, answering the two vital questions ("what" and "how") with style and knowledge, with Prose finding a form for answering both questions that accomplishes the task with great creativity.

The review is five pages in length, and Prose uses every line of space available to her without ever letting a single line appear extraneous or go leaden. Prose's prose fairly rings off the page. Her creativity reveals itself most readily in the structure of her review: the review takes the form of a musical piece in four "movements," the first movement accomplishing initial answering of the question, What is the book about? The second movement takes comparable preliminary steps in answering the question, How good is it? The third and fourth movements address the two questions—in the same order—in more specific terms.

In the first movement, Prose looks at one particular short story written by the great Russian master of the form, Isaac Babel: a story entitled "My Fat Goose." After her brief but certainly enticing synopsis of this story, she then recalls being read the entire story by her college writing instructor, back in 1966, and she remembers distinctly her reactions back then to Babel's trenchant writing. Because she can—because she has the room in this long review to do so—Prose spends three long but nevertheless quite absorbing paragraphs filling her reader in on major events and themes in the life of Isaac Babel, who died prematurely in 1939 at the hands of the Soviet police.

Thus ends the review's first movement. This represents Prose's initial answer to one of the two vital questions answered in *all* reviews: What is the book about? Her answer takes the form, in this first part of the review, of her sharing her first encounter with Babel's fiction in college, which is followed by a biographical rundown on the writer.

At this point, Prose skillfully and gracefully moves into the How good is it? portion of her review, with this two-part statement: "Novelists, poets, and serious readers speak of his work with an intense—and almost cultlike—respect and devotion. So why is Babel's work not widely known, nor his name universally recognized, among the literate public?"[3]

Then begins the second movement of the review. As Prose did in her initial step toward eventually offering a full answer to What is the book about? she now offers a preliminary answer to the question, How good is it? Prose sensitively analyzes the quality of Babel's writing, structuring her response around the question she asked of why Babel is not well known to the "literate" reading public. Two major points in her support of Babel's distinctiveness center on the fact that "countless writers have linked sex and death, violence and art, but few have made that linkage appear so raw and unromantic";[4] and "it is hard to think of a writer of equal genius whose work runs so directly counter to the prevailing popular taste for sympathetic characters and an affirmative worldview."[5]

HOOPER'S REVIEWS

Love in the Time of Cholera,
by Gabriel García Márquez,
tr. by Edith Grossman (Knopf, 1988)

The Colombian-born Nobel laureate, author of the internationally celebrated *One Hundred Years of Solitude* (1970), has produced another splendid work of fiction, one that may come to be fondly reread more than *Solitude,* as it is far more accessible. It is an exquisite love story, set in an unnamed Latin American location. The eminent physician, Dr. Juvenal Urbino de la Calle, has passed away, leaving behind a bereft but still vital widow, Fermina Daza. Upon the death of Fermina's husband, a man emerges out of her past, Florentino Ariza, with whom she was involved before her marriage, more than five decades ago. He declares his continued love of Fermina, and what happens to the two of them after that declaration proves the wisdom of García Márquez's closing lines: "It is life, more than death, that has no limits." These characters are deeply, intricately drawn and utterly fascinating. The poetry of the author's style, the humor of his voice, the joyous detail in which the plot is upholstered—all are reasons to live in this lush, luxurious novel as long as you desire. García Márquez consistently eschews economy of presentation; he practices a kind of studied indirection, with entrancing digressions into characters' past lives, but the narrative is perfectly followable; it builds slowly, deliberately, but in a way ponderously. This is a beautiful story, beautifully told, and it should not be missed by any reader of literary fiction.

Booklist, February 1, 1988

So Prose establishes the worth of Babel, the reasons for his greatness, and then artfully slips back into answering, more roundly this second time, the question of what the book is about. This is the third movement of the musical composition, as it were. This time she specifically illuminates for the reader what exactly *is* the book at hand: in this case, a volume that for the first time gathers between two covers all of the work of this significant, consequential Russian writer—not only his short stories but also his plays, screenplays, sketches, essays, and other fragments and occasional pieces. The book, as Prose notes, runs to nearly one thousand pages: a monument, then, to Babel's importance.

Quite imaginatively and successfully in terms of the readability of the review, Prose then returns to the issue of how good the book is. Why she chooses to do so is because this book begs a second, and ultimately more important, answer to that question. And that centers on the translation.

This complete edition of Babel's work has been newly translated for this occasion, and Prose is intimately familiar with how Babel read in his previous translation; so, for her, comparisons are natural and inevitable. And she finds this new rendering from Russian into English quite lacking. In fact, she cannot be described as anything but appalled when she concludes that "one can hardly bear to imagine how Isaac Babel might regard the awkwardness, the clichés, and the inexactitude of the language in which he is now being presented in English."[6]

How appropriately conceived and structured is this review! First is an introduction to Isaac Babel as a story writer that imparts the fundamental facts of his life; then comes Prose's glowing assessment of his work. Next is a specific discussion about what the book contains and its specialness in that regard. Finally, Prose offers a very critical assessment of the book's primary feature—that it is a new translation. In this fourth and concluding movement is borne the major point and thrust of the review: that despite Prose having nothing but good to say about Babel, this inadequate translation reduces his impact.

This kind of full, complete review needs to run to several pages in length—which indeed it does.

But what the short review in *Booklist* and the much longer one in *Harper's* share is their having accomplished their basic task: to answer the two questions every review must supply an answer to: What is this book about? How good is it?

HOW TO DETERMINE WHAT A NONFICTION BOOK IS ABOUT

How does someone who is reviewing a book determine what the book is about? Generally speaking, it is easier to discern the answer to that question when dealing with a nonfiction book; it is usually a relatively straightforward process in identifying the topic of a nonfiction book, at least in basic terms.

If the review book at hand is a nonfiction book whose subject matter cannot, after the first chapters, be comprehended, and the argument the author is pursuing is neither apparent nor comprehensible by then, one of two problems is certain to exist. First, the book is beyond the reviewer's scope of reference and familiarity, and consequently he or she should quietly put the book down, to leave for a reviewer with more background. Second, if a reader possessing a workable familiarity with the book's topic—at least based on preliminary perusal of its jacket copy—cannot understand what the author is up to by the end of the first chapter, then the book should also be set down by the reviewer. In such a case, the question of how good the book is has been answered: not good at all—so bad, in fact, it can't be reviewed by anyone.

To reiterate, answering the question of what a book is about is usually a neat process with a nonfiction book, if the book is making itself readily understood and the reviewer is not at sea with the topic at hand. A book on the theory of relativity, for instance, will be readily identified as such, in general terms; but a more specific identification of its content and purpose will depend on the depth of the reviewer's own fundamental familiarity with the subject or the ease with which the author communicates his subject to reviewers with little or no previous experience with or exposure to the book's topic.

HOW TO DECIDE HOW GOOD THE NONFICTION BOOK IS

When a reviewer seeks an answer to the second vital question the review must answer—How good is the book?—the reviewer must first ponder two considerations: Is the book for the *general* reader? Or is it for the *specialized* reader? A book for the specialized reader on, say, the Russian

Revolution is to be judged by the criteria of academic scholarship, and reviews of that kind of book will more likely appear in scholarly journals, where a considerable reading background on the part of the person reading the review is prescribed. And the reviewer, of course, will have a background in academe or at least full familiarity with the scholarly literature on the subject.

For a book addressed to the general reader on the same topic—the Russian Revolution—reviewers must keep in mind an essential factor when asking themselves how good the book in hand is: Does the reader learn the basic facts about the event—what happened, why it happened, who caused it to happen—and does the reader learn those vital areas of information in a fluid, well-ordered presentation, or does the reader have to struggle with the author to gain this necessary information?

This is, then, the major question in determining how good a nonfiction book is: Does the reader learn the essential facts, or at least the essential points the author is trying to make, and learn them easily and comfortably? Or at least, with close attention paid, does the reader learn them without too large a degree of tussle with the author?

HOW TO DETERMINE WHAT NOVELS ARE ABOUT (AND HOW GOOD THEY ARE)

Determining what a novel is about and how good it is presents a more challenging exercise. Let us take a famous novel as an example—a famous novel most people will have read or at least seen the film version of, *Gone with the Wind* (*GWTW*). (Remember that in chapter 2, *GWTW* is used to demonstrate positive or negative extremes in reviewing the same book.)

What is *Gone with the Wind* about? "It's about the Civil War" would be the reviewer's first response. But novels, even historical novels, are always—usually always *should* be—about characters first and foremost; who they are and what they do form the basis of most novels.

So, keeping that maxim in mind, we could more truthfully, more specifically say that *Gone with the Wind* is about a spoiled, vain, selfish young woman. That certainly is not an elusive perception to have arrived at. But does a twelve-step procedure exist for determining what a novel is about, like a key by which, as in analyzing a leaf (if you recall high-school biology), the kind of tree it came from can be identified?

No, of course not. Is anything in life that easy? The ability for such determining comes from *experience* in reading novels, reading more novels, and then reading even more novels. Just as you cannot be a good novelist without vast experience reading novels, you also cannot be a good reviewer of novels without considerable experience in reading novels—to see more than just what the surface of a novel tells you.

THE FIVE ELEMENTS OF FICTION

Here is a little plan for determining what a novel is about, one that will place the reviewer in a good position for answering the question, How good is it?

The plan is simple: remember the five basic elements of fiction:

1. Characters
2. Plot
3. Theme
4. Setting
5. Style

Characters, Plot, and Theme

The first questions to ask yourself when reviewing a novel are, Who are the characters, and what do they do? Answer those questions and you are off and running in writing a review of a novel.

Experience, then, informs you that *Gone with the Wind*, in terms of character, is about a spoiled, selfish woman who focuses exclusively on her own needs in a time of great national distress—in this case, the Civil War—and exploits these difficult times for everyone not simply to save herself from hardship but also to actually advance herself economically.

Woven tightly into the element of character in a novel are the accompanying elements of plot and theme. As previously mentioned, who the characters are in a novel and what they do form the raw material of most novels. Scarlett O'Hara was a daughter of the privileged white Southern landowning class, a woman whose traits and tribulations reflect not only her unabashed tenacity but also, in a much broader sense, serve as a paradigm of the struggle of her class to regain a foothold while having to endure the privations of war, the burden and stigma of conquest by the enemy, and the ignominy of Reconstruction.

This is the framework around which Margaret Mitchell constructed her timeless American novel. But you can see that when identifying the main character and relating, however briefly, the gist of what happened to her, we have indicated in very general terms the story line of the novel—the plot—and at the same time suggested the "definition" of the plot. The plot's "definition" constitutes what can be identified as the theme of the novel, which, in this case, we would say was how a vain, superficial, manipulative young woman gains strength in the face of not only personal but also national calamity—however, she uses her newfound strength to continue to manipulate the people around her and exploit the insecure circumstances in which they all find themselves.

Thus, the concepts of character, plot, and theme are inexorably tied to one another; one means nothing without the other. What a character does *is* the plot; how and why the character does what she or he does, basically speaking, is the theme. (The latter includes family dysfunction, man against the elements, a stranger comes to town, a person goes on a long voyage, and the agonies and ecstasies of love, to name a few.)

Theme is not always easily defined. Nevertheless, theme is greatly important in readers' advisory work. Whether library patrons realize it, they actually cite the theme of a novel they have just read when they explain to the librarian why they liked a certain novel and plead for the librarian to find them another one "just like it."

Setting

Two other factors are of major significance in a novel—two vital "systems," if we may exercise another metaphor: the novel as an advanced living organism—and by which fiction is properly judged: setting and style. A novel's setting, which is defined as the time and place in which the action takes place, may be underplayed by the author as only the barest stage upon which the plot rests and is developed. That is often the case in a novel that is primarily character driven, because most of what the author is interested in presenting is a probe into the dimensions of a character's psychology.

Still, even in a novel that is indeed clearly a character study, where and when the character or characters are facing the events that come their way need to be anchored at least in some small degree in a time and a place so as to give the reader a decent share of foundation upon which to accept the reality of the plot. This is true even if the novel is fantasy or strictly a metaphor, which will have its own reality.

So, no matter how minimal the setting, no matter where and when the action takes place—even if it is an interior novel, one that takes place inside a character's head—to judge the total quality of a novel, the reader must ask if the setting is accurate to its time and place. At the very least, does it give the distinct feel of time and place? Ask yourself this when judging setting: Has the author given the feel of a time and place? The reader need not be an authority on that particular setting to determine this. For example, historical novels as well as novels written about contemporary times are set in environments different from every reader's experiences. Not only must the setting ring authentic—historical plausibility, as Italian novelist Nino Ricco calls it, if you are talking about a historical novel—it must add dimension to the story being told, and it must enhance the story's resonance.

As noted, if the novel is an "interior" type, in which setting is kept to the barest of outline, the reviewer must ask himself or herself, Does the author's choice work? Is only the skimpiest of detail about when and where the character is either prompting or reacting to events a more effective way of emphasizing characterization? Or does it seem the author simply paid inadequate attention to that aspect of the story, and consequently, the reader is unavoidably left with an inadequate foundation from which to gain a full appreciation of the character and his or her plight? A character undergoing the experiences and changes that the author has set out for that individual to go through cannot float entirely in space without somewhat of a time-and-place foundation. It rests on the talent of the author to determine whether minimal foundation is sufficient for the reader to truly, fully appreciate the truths about human nature the author wishes to convey in the creation of his character. The universality of those particular traits—the applicability to all humans—ironically has to be tied, at least in some fashion, however loosely, to a place and time for us to believe in the relevance of their truths. They have to be true about someone in a certain setting, no matter how vaguely sketched that setting is, for those truths to resonate and make us believe they can be true about anyone in any setting.

These are the aspects of setting by which novels are judged. Does it ring authentic, and is it developed sufficiently for the author's purposes? Does it add dimension to the story being told rather than detract from or diminish it?

Style

Style, a personal, subjective issue, is by far the most slippery quality by which a novel can be evaluated.

Basically, an author's writing style will be perceived by the reader as either smooth or bumpy, like a highway: getting you where you want to go without your being conscious of the pavement beneath you, or being conscious of the pavement because it is not a smooth, unobtrusive surface.

But to judge whether the pavement—the writing style—is smooth or bumpy remains a subjective enterprise, for a style that is deemed intrusive by one reader—a bumpy pavement that detracts from the reading experience, that interrupts the reader's appreciation of the story and the characters—may just be another reader's added positive reading experience. The latter enjoys the author's purposely created bumps in the road, sensing the bumps as heightened texture to the reader's journey.

Raymond Carver's Prose

Let me repeat: defining, then judging, the quality of an author's writing style is a very subjective call. For example, many readers and critics as well have paid tribute to the bare-bones writing style of the late, famous short-story writer Raymond Carver, the fountainhead of the so-called minimalist school of fiction writing that remained quite in vogue throughout the 1980s and into the early 1990s. Here is an example of Carver's distinctive, much-imitated style, a passage taken from his story "Neighbors," which appeared in his first collection, *Will You Please Be Quiet, Please?* (1976):

> The Stones lived across the hall from the Millers. Jim was a salesman for a machine-parts firm and often managed to combine business with pleasure trips, and on this occasion the Stones would be

> away from home ten days, first to Cheyenne, then on to St. Louis to visit relatives. In their absence, the Millers would look after the Stones' apartment, feed Kitty, and water the plants.
>
> Bill and Jim shook hands beside the car. Harriet and Arlene held each other by the elbows and kissed lightly on the lips.
>
> "Have fun," Bill said to Harriet.
>
> "We will," said Harriet. "You kids have fun, too."
>
> Arlene nodded.
>
> Jim winked at her. "Bye, Arlene. Take good care of the old man."
>
> "I will," Arlene said.[7]

Carver employs the barest of detail, with one simple sentence standing in for lots of information that Carver chooses only to suggest. Focus specifically, for instance, on the line: "Jim was a salesman for a machine-parts firm and often managed to combine business with pleasure trips." Nothing more is said than that, and that is sufficient information to set the context for this particular trip out of town, during which the neighbors, the Millers, would keep an eye on Jim and Harriet's house.

The dialogue is sparse and direct. Carver's characters are people of only the most necessary of words. These non-language-oriented people Carver writes about speak, like many people, by simply exchanging required greetings and information, not employing oratorical flourishes in any fashion.

Carver's style is perfect for his intent, then, and should be judged perfect for the occasion.

Reynolds Price's Prose

In contrast to Raymond Carver, here is a passage from a novel entitled *The Promise of Rest* (1995), written by the contemporary and highly regarded (both critically and popularly) southern fiction writer Reynolds Price:

> Hutch was watching his father, no move to rise. He knew he was waiting for an urgent choice to be made on his life; he knew his father was the one who could make it—that his own strong body, for all its rush to fullness, was in the hands of others and would be for years yet. Might always be (he had had no taste of freedom in life or dreams).
>
> Rob said "Invite me here to live."
>
> "This house?" Hutch said.

"Just at first. We could move to the Kendal place by fall."

"We and who?" Hutch said.

"Grainger maybe. Maybe Min."

Hutch met his eyes, asking. They were genuinely asking Hutch for some gift at last. But he knew he couldn't give it. It was not his to give; it had not grown in him yet. Still he didn't say that, didn't say, "I'm still a boy. Nothing in me understands you." He shook his head. "No, sir." Then he stood and went to the chair where his clothes lay and turned his back to Rob.[8]

Price is occasionally criticized for an "ornateness" of style and an "unlikeliness" in his dialogue, in part because he most often deals with characters drawn from the small town and rural areas of his native North Carolina. Regardless, who cannot help but enjoy the lushness of his language as, in this example, a young-man son negotiates with his father from the perspective of not being adult enough to make the kind of decision his father is asking him to make? What a beautiful line is this: "that his own strong body, for all its rush to fullness, was in the hands of others and would be for years yet."

HOOPER'S REVIEWS

American Lion: Andrew Jackson in the White House, by Jon Meacham (Random House, 2008)

There are numerous books on the seventh president, but this one is distinguished by its particularly fluid presentation. As the subtitle indicates, it has special appeal for those readers who may be uninterested in a complete cradle-to-grave treatment but are looking for a particular focus on the Jackson presidency. The "evolution of presidential power" is the basic theme around which Meacham constructs his riveting account of the freshness Jackson brought to the White House—meaning, before his advent into the chief executive office, political power was considered to be best left in the hands of the landed elite, but Jackson believed in the "primacy of the will of the [common] people," and during his administration, "democracy was making its stand." This was a difficult time for the American republic; the issue of slavery was developing into a major political issue, and with that, the rise of southern questioning of just how strong the union of states was and what rights individual states possessed to safeguard regional interests. But Jackson administered the ship of state with good instincts and wisdom.

Booklist, November 15, 2008

Price's dialogue gives his characters a definite eloquence, but not really an unnatural eloquence, for in every one of his novels, he creates a culture in which the most ordinary of people tap into a culturewide ability to speak, not with the flatness we associate with Raymond Carver, but with conscious word choice to express themselves concisely but resonantly.

As different as night is from day—the ways Raymond Carver and Reynolds Price present both dialogue and description. Is one way the correct way? Absolutely not. There are questions to ponder: Is a simpler style used effectively in this writer's hands, or does it come across as arid? Conversely but concomitantly, is the much more elaborate style employed by the other writer an effective or labored use of rich language?

This represents the part of reviewing in which the reviewer's taste must be separated from judging a piece of writing. Reviewers tend to prefer one or the other: a more plainspoken style or a more complicated one. But it is the duty of reviewers to set aside their personal partiality and judge the style of a writer on its own merits: its effectiveness in conveying the story line and character-building process as either the smoothest of pavements to let the story line and character building speak only for themselves or as a deeply textured pavement adding to the reader's response to the writer's prose.

If the simple style or the most elaborate style calls too much attention to itself, to the point of distracting the reader away from the nuances, subtleties, and steps in the structuring of characters, then the reviewer has every reason—every right—to criticize the writing style.

Ernest Hemingway's Prose

Let me showcase two more, quite disparate writing styles. The first is from a giant of twentieth-century literature, Nobel Prize winner Ernest Hemingway, whose writing, to me, is maddeningly, self-consciously pared down and, consequently, does exactly what I have warned against: it draws too much attention to itself for me to react to it as anything other than an obstacle to my total appreciation of Hemingway's writing:

> "You see, Nick, babies are supposed to be born head first but sometime they're not. When they're not they make a lot of trouble for everybody. Maybe I'll have to operate on this lady. We'll know in a little while."

When he was satisfied with his hands he went in and went to work.

"Pull back that quilt, will you, George?" he said. "I'd rather not touch it."

Later when he started to operate Uncle George and three Indian men held the woman still. She bit Uncle George on the arm and Uncle George said, "Damn squaw bitch!" and the young Indian who had rowed Uncle George over laughed at him. Nick held the basin for his father. It all took a long time.

His father picked the baby up and slapped it to make it breathe and handed it to the old woman.

"See, it's a boy, Nick," he said. "How do you like being an interne?"

Nick said, "All right." He was looking away so as not to see what his father was doing.[9]

The preceding passage is from a famous story, "Indian Camp," found in the collection *In Our Time* (1924) by the American literary god Hemingway, as famous in his day for his stripped-down style as Raymond Carver was in a latter day. Hemingway's prose, while unembroidered, unfettered, and unadorned, is, in many people's eyes, beautiful in its sheerness, a stiletto blow between the ribs, a face slap. To these readers, his prose delivers much pungency very quickly.

Elizabeth Bowen's Prose

Now, here is a sample of the work of fiction writer Elizabeth Bowen that is much the opposite from Hemingway's but beautiful in its decorativeness:

Obliteration of everything by winter was to be dreaded. Already the late-autumnal closing in of the evenings was setting a term to new adventures; their scene was vanishing—some sort of mindless hope had gone on haunting her for just so long as daylight had gone on haunting streets. Through the summer her husband's step, still only just out of hearing, could be imagined turning and coming back; while summer lasted she therefore still need not shut up shop. Within the narrowing of autumn, the impulses of incredulous loneliness died down in her; among them that readiness to quicken which had made her look for her husband in other faces. True, she felt nearer Tom with any man than she did with no man—true love is to be recognized by its aberrations; so shocking can these be, so inexplicable to any other person, that true love is seldom to be recognized at all.[10]

This paragraph is taken from a novel entitled *The Heat of the Day* (1949), by Anglo-Irish novelist and short-story writer Bowen, a writer I enjoy for her distinctly arresting prose. Read the paragraph again, aloud this time—and slowly. Bowen's talent for achingly resonant metaphors makes you want to sing an aria to creative language that doesn't simply communicate but does it in a soaring fashion. Is not "the late-autumnal closing in of the evenings" a lovely, fresh, creative way to describe dusk? And the repetition of the word *haunting* in "some sort of mindless hope had gone on haunting her for just so long as daylight had gone on haunting streets" sets up a solid image that the use of the word only once would not quite have accomplished, and at the same time, the repetition does not strike the reader as the least clumsy or accidental on the author's part. Such is Bowen's talent: knowing the effectiveness of repetition to complete a metaphor.

What a lovely as well as wise observation about life she expresses in the line: "true love is to be recognized by its aberrations; so shocking can these be, so inexplicable to any other person, that true love is seldom to be recognized at all."

Bowen's style, as far as I am concerned, only enhances the unfolding of the story and the creation of her characters as well as the expression of her view of the world, rather than detracts from it. The reader certainly must travel slowly down the highway of her prose, to pay attention to her artful language usage, but that is all part of the total appreciation of Bowen and the magnificent writer she is.

So, in judging a writer's style, taste plays an awfully important role in the evaluation process; nevertheless, the reviewer needs to back up his or her assertions and defenses of taste with example justifications—however brief, sometimes just a phrase sufficing—to support the opinion as to why the style does or does not work to best serve the author's needs.

In truth, if a reviewer is so absolutely opposed to a writer's style to the point of inability to see around his or her personal aversion to it, then that reviewer should give the book up, to be reviewed by someone else.

But another truth of the matter is, a good reviewer is open to all manners of style and reacts to each kind of style on a case-by-case basis. That point leads us to discussing what makes a good review, which we will take up in the following chapter.

NOTES

1. Mark Knoblauch, review of *Comfort Me with Apples: More Adventures at the Table*, by Ruth Reichl, *Booklist* 97 (April 1, 2001): 1427.

2. Ibid.

3. Francine Prose, "The Bones of Muzhiks," review of *The Complete Works of Isaac Babel*, by Isaac Babel, *Harper's Magazine* 303 (November 2001): 75.

4. Ibid.

5. Ibid., 76.

6. Ibid., 79.

7. Raymond Carver, "Neighbors," in *Will You Please Be Quiet, Please?* (New York: Vintage, 1976), 9.

8. Reynolds Price, *The Promise of Rest* (New York: Atheneum, 1995), 348–349.

9. Ernest Hemingway, "Indian Camp," in *In Our Time* (Scribner, 1924), 17.

10. Elizabeth Bowen, *The Heat of the Day* (New York: Penguin, 1949), 145.

WHAT MAKES A GOOD REVIEW? 5

W e have explored the questions of what is in a review. Now we can take the discussion to the next level and address the characteristics of a good review as opposed to simply a decent one.

CHARACTERISTICS OF A GOOD REVIEW

Be Lively

First and foremost, a good review is *lively*. Leaden prose is a killer no matter if it is found in a review or in any other piece of writing. Unfortunately, boring writing works a double danger in a review: it leaves the reader uninterested in finishing the review as well as runs the risk of causing the reader's disinterest in reading the book itself, even if the review is positive.

Does *lively* imply *humorous*? One can mean the other, certainly, but not necessarily. Humor in a review should always be appropriate—and its appropriateness usually means that the book itself is humorous, and thus one of the points the reviewer hopes to express is sharing the book's humorous tone.

That brings us to an interesting general point—a basic precept of good reviewing—about the correlation between the tone of a book and the tone of the review. A good, complete review, even a brief 175-word review, will indicate the tone of a book. The tone can be spelled out in so many words. That indeed works. But also—more artfully and arguably more effectively—the tone can be introduced and reinforced in the reader's mind by the review re-creating that tone itself. But this should not be attempted sloppily or without full forethought.

A humorous book can be reviewed humorously. But care should be taken that the humor is not strained, that the reviewer is not competing with the book in achieving a sense of humor. On the other hand, a book on a serious subject, such as domestic abuse, obviously is best reviewed in a correlatively serious tone. A book about refurbishing a house in Tuscany can, and should, be reviewed not necessarily lightheartedly but certainly in a tone that conveys the romance anyone would feel when even imagining what it would be like to establish oneself in a villa in the hills above Florence.

Having your review *reflect* the tone of the book under consideration—as opposed to simply *stating* what the tone is—is a subtle art. Practiced well, it contributes nuance and depth to a review; clumsily done, it draws attention to itself and to the reviewer, just like writing in an overwrought style wrongly removes the focus from the book and onto the reviewer (see "No Overwriting Allowed," in chapter 6). Correlating the tone of a review and the tone of the book is almost an instinctual ability, one that the reviewer cannot be overly conscious of when writing the review or it will appear too obvious and thus too clumsy. Ability to subtly plant the tone of a book into the review comes from experience. Remember our maxim about being a good reviewer? *Experience, experience, experience.*

Below, quoted in full, is a review I wrote that appeared in 2001 in *Booklist*. It exhibits, so I trust, a good incorporation of tone into content: in this case, having fun with a book on cars that will certainly evoke a warm, wonderful sense of nostalgia:

> **Willson, Quentin. *Cars: A Celebration*. Sept. 2001. 576p. illus. DK, $50 (0-7894-8155-3).**
>
> Oh, the hours that car lovers will pore over the bold, dramatic pages of this large-format celebration of automobile types and styles found around the world in recent decades. Arrangement is alphabetical by marque, from the AC Ace-Bristol (a British roadster of the late 1950s) to the Willys Jeep MB (the workhorse used by the military in World War II). For each kind of featured car, a complete profile is offered: a brief history and a rundown on statistics in chart form as well as a series of luscious, crystal-clear photographs taken of the car from the front, back, top, and—across two-page spreads—side. Yes, the Edsel might have been a consumer failure, but its laughed-at styling nevertheless

now seems very typical of the fifties. But laugh at the Lamborghini of the 1970s? And let's not even get started on how we ache to have owned a Corvette Sting Ray. And remember the neighbor in the 1970s who used to collect 1959 Cadillacs? To dream . . .[1]

Be Serious

A review of a book on a very serious subject should reflect the book's seriousness and not be flip or arch. This situation, however, does not preclude liveliness. A review can be serious without being deadly dull. A reviewer can choose energetic words and create strong, vigorous, vital sentences without lack of respect for the book's seriousness. In fact, if the review reeks of—overstates—the book's seriousness, the reviewer risks the reader assuming that the book, or at least the book's author, is being mocked. A mocking tone is rarely supportable in a review, or excusable only if a book is very bad and the reviewer is definitely not recommending it (but see "Avoid Negative Reviewing," below). Consequently, mocking it is the least barbed way of getting the negative point across— but even then, a mocking tone is questionable.

No Place for Condescension

A discussion about tone must include this dictum: there is no place in any review for condescension.

For example, here is a hypothetical reviewer statement that can only be taken by the reader as condescension:

> This kind of action novel is simple to write and simple to read, and there are many readers out there who need the sort of mindless diversion this novel provides.

Here is the same basic judgment expressed without either overt or implied condemnation:

> This action novel is easy to follow and thus appropriate for readers interested in entertaining and not especially challenging diversionary reading.

Reviewers who habitually write with a condescending attitude often are not aware of it. Condescension in critical appraisal customarily reflects condescension toward the entire universe. Frankly, it is a dangerous situation; it will be the rare review this person writes into which condescension has not insidiously crept.

Milquetoasts Not Allowed

Even more insidious is the reviewer who is a timid person, intimidated or even threatened by the world, and who feels he or she is not being noted by the world at large and has little power to exert control over anything. If this sort of personality sits down to write a review, too often this pent-up need for power will emerge between the lines or even in the specific language of the review. What emerges is often sarcasm. Seen within this context, a negative stand toward a book—without justifiable reasons, that is—is a form of control, of the reviewer putting herself or himself in a position of exerting power.

So, a good review is lively and written in a secure voice, one that indicates the reviewer is in command of the material in a book or audiobook,

---

HOOPER'S REVIEWS

Cheever, by Blake Bailey (Knopf, 2009)

John Cheever is not widely read anymore. In his day during the 1950s and 1960s, his short stories appeared regularly in the *New Yorker*, and when his first novel, the long-labored-over *Wapshot Chronicle*, was published in 1957, he achieved recognition as one of the foremost American fiction writers. Now his stories, upon which his reputation had been based and several of which are universally regarded as masterpieces of the form, are no longer read even in college-level literature or creative-writing courses. Perhaps a Cheever renaissance of sorts will result from this magnificently understanding and understandable biography based on copious research and destined to be the definitive life treatment for many years to come. To hold up his life as a perfect example of that of the tortured artist would not be a mistake. Seen here, Cheever had troubled relationships with his family, which haunted him forever; wrestled with his abhorred homosexual tendencies all his adult life; and developed into a desperate alcoholic. His various therapists found him to be a narcissistic personality riddled with self-doubt, and from the detailed picture composed here, the reader can only concur. Riveting from page 1, this is the literary biography of the season and will be talked about for years to come; it will also, it is hoped, guide readers once again to his distinctive fiction, especially his short stories.

Booklist, November 1, 2008

whether it be a nonfiction title on the human genome or a novel about human frailties. The reviewer's voice must be firm as it supplies answers to the two vital questions needing answer in any review: What is the book or audiobook about? How good is it? Equivocation in answering the two crucial questions is not permitted.

NO LECTURING, PLEASE

Just as a reviewer should avoid condescension, reviewers should also avoid, even while exercising their authoritative voice, a lecturing voice. If reviewers are in a lecturing mode, enjoying hearing their own voices as they recite fact after fact or spew out what they feel are priceless but endless nuggets of information, all the while editorializing about this, that, and the other thing, who wants to finish reading the review? The reader is bound to think: life is too short; let's go on to something else.

For an example of what I am talking about, take this quote from— again—a hypothetical review:

> James Polk should not be overlooked as president. Although he served only one term, 1845–1849, he succeeded in all the goals and objectives he set out to accomplish. He is buried on the grounds of the Statehouse in Nashville. Presidential tombs make fascinating tourist objectives; you can travel just through the Midwest and see some interesting ones. My favorite is Warren Harding's tomb in Marion, Ohio.

Certainly, any reviewer should deliver firm opinions about the book or audiobook, but those opinions are best not delivered in a lecturing tone, as if the reviewer were Teddy Roosevelt standing at the bully pulpit. No one likes being lectured to, and that includes being lectured to as to whether you should or should not read a certain book or listen to a certain audiobook.

Here is another made-up example, which illustrates my point about shouting:

> This topic can't be written about enough. It's the major sociological issue of our day. No responsible citizen can ignore the significance and potential ramifications of it. If unchecked, the situation could mean the end of life as we know it. Ignore this book at your own risk!

The reader of the review can only think about the reviewer: "Oh, settle down!"

Enthusiasm is a wonderful commodity to share, and the more enthusiastic a reviewer is about a book, the more it indeed should be shared, but shared in vibrant, expressive language, not in a high or loud or feverish pitch. People hate being forced to listen to someone; they will listen much better, and learn far easier, from someone who is obviously enthusiastic but speaks—or writes—in even, comfortable, tempered tones.

Don't talk down, don't lecture, don't pound and shout. Smooth and easy go it best.

THE QUESTION OF APPLES AND ORANGES

A good review, too, is a review that judges a book only against others of its ilk, that is, judges apples against other apples, not against oranges. This may seem an obvious concept, but the problem does indeed arise, especially with reviewers wanting to prove themselves. And one way reviewers attempt this is by insisting the book in their hands is no match against some previous book—but the problem is, the book under review is not *intended* by the author to occupy the same niche as the previous book the reviewer has in mind.

In specific terms, then, a good reviewer of the latest novel by romance writer Danielle Steel will not be comparing this nevertheless very popular writer to the social dramas of the great literary goddess Edith Wharton. Danielle Steel most certainly is not trying to be a latter-day Edith Wharton; the two authors are, indeed, apples and oranges. To actually point out in a review that Steel is not Wharton is not only silly, pompous, and smacking of neophytism but also a waste of precious reviewing space.

No one reading the review would expect anyone to speak of Danielle Steel and Edith Wharton in the same breath. What the reviewer intends to be submitting to the reader as astute criticism actually comes across as the opposite: insipid, unnecessary, and inexperienced. Danielle Steel is to be compared to herself—where does her latest novel fit into her oeuvre in terms of setting, theme, and the level of quality of her storytelling as established in previous books?—and compared to other romance writers, particularly compared to others in the top level of romance writing.

Let us say a reviewer has in his or her hands a biography of the god-composer Wolfgang Mozart. It is a volume in the Penguin Lives series, the purpose of which is to provide general readers with fresh, new, compact introductions to the lives of important figures in all walks of life, past and present. Yes, the good reviewer undoubtedly will compare it to other biographical treatments of Mozart, but only to indicate if general features in Mozart's life are being differently interpreted in this new series entry in the Penguin Lives books—not to criticize this new book for being only an overview. The only true comparison a reviewer could make is to compare it to some other books having the purpose of introducing Mozart's life.

Oranges must not be compared to apples, but neither should oranges be compared to tangerines.

LIKABLE PROTAGONISTS OR NOT

Another interesting topic falls into the bigger category of the components of a good review. Reviewers often ask, Is it valid to dismiss a novel because the reviewer doesn't like the main character? Many readers believe a novel can't totally succeed without a likable main character.

It is enough to simply *understand* the main character, regardless of liking him or her. And if that proves to be the case, then there should at least be *some* characters in the cast to like.

Here is a trenchant quote on the subject, in a review appearing in the *New York Times Book Review* of Diane Johnson's novel *Lulu in Marrakech:* "There's no law that says a novel's central character has to be appealing or likable, no matter what the book clubs tell us."[2]

But once again, subjectivity rears its difficult head. A character one reader likes could easily be a character another reader does *not* like. That said, if an author sets out to make the main character unlikable, this character should very much be made understandable at the same time, and among the supporting characters there definitely should be some that are likable or at least sympathetic.

Thus, a reviewer can criticize a novel for not presenting a likable main character or not enough likable characters, but on the other hand, the reviewer must be careful not to dismiss a novel as "not good" because of that. If, however, the characterization process is faulty—the way an author builds up a character into a credible human being, whether an admirable one or a less-than-noble one by any stretch of the imagination—then that is a different story, and the author deserves strong criticism.

AVOID NEGATIVE REVIEWING

Though strong criticism can be leveled at the author for flawed characterization, for example, reviewers should avoid negative reviewing: stating in a review that a book is not good at all and should not be bothered with—that is, neither should it be read nor selected for library purchase.

Certainly reviewers can offer some negative comments about a book or audiobook in a review that turns out to be overall a recommendation to read the book or, if you are a librarian involved in book selection for your library, to purchase the item for the library collection.

In most instances, review editors consider negative reviews unpublishable. All review venues struggle against page-budget constraints. Newspapers, for example, depend on advertising revenues to "pay for" the editorial content. As advertisers choose different venues, newspapers (and other publications tied to advertising funds) must reduce their size. Hence, review sections in Sunday newspapers are shrinking. So, the reasoning goes, why consume space to tell readers *not* to read a certain book or listen to a certain audiobook (and lose the potential advertising dollars)? Isn't it better, financially and editorially, to use available space reviewing recommended materials?

Generally, the answer is yes. But as in most aspects of life, the truth lies in a gray area. What about books by major writers? What if a reviewer thinks the latest book by a major writer doesn't work; should he or she simply not review it? Or what if the reviewer finds he or she does not care for the review item at all, but because of the "hot" topic or the celebrity author, the book will be hyped in the press and talked about on the morning talk shows? Reviewed, then?

These questions are important concerns in reviewing, and they demarcate the gray area of the issue of negative reviewing. It really would not be fair to let a major writer off the hook for writing a bad book simply because he or she *is* a major writer, right? And major writers are indeed capable of writing bad books. So, shouldn't the emperor be told he is wearing no clothes? Absolutely.

Negative reviewing consumes valuable reviewing space and should be practiced sparingly and thoughtfully. It should be reserved for material by major figures and materials on hot topics bound to be much discussed in the press. As a general rule, books that turn out to be not so good should not be reviewed; instead, review a book you are happy with and want people to see for themselves whether they like it.

An Example of Negative Reviewing

Let me cite an excellent example of an occasion when a negative review is not only worthwhile but practically necessary. This review is by a favorite book reviewer of mine, Walter Kirn, the former literary editor at *GQ* magazine, and the book he is reviewing is a novel by the once-avant-garde and widely noted John Barth titled *Coming Soon!!!* John Barth is not exactly a household name, but his reputation remains high

HOOPER'S REVIEWS

The Tenth Muse: My Life in Food, by Judith Jones (Knopf, 2007)

In her entertaining, wondrously informative remembrance of her rich life, written with not a paragraph or even a word of pretension or boastfulness, cookbook editor Jones recounts experiences that food and book lovers will admire and envy and, when the book is finished, wish took up twice as many pages. Jones reaches back into her childhood for clear memories of signs and indications that food and its preparation would always be a source of delight. Clearly woven into her remembrances, like a bright thread, is her abiding interest in things French; in fact, after college, she journeyed there and took up long-term residence, meeting the man who would become her husband and absorbing the Gallic delight in scents and sauces. Once back living in New York, she worked as an editor at Knopf, sort of falling into editing cookbooks. Her crowning achievement was the acquisition of the manuscript to what would be called *Mastering the Art of French Cooking*, by the unknown Julia Child. Other important cookbook acquisitions followed, reflecting America's growing sophistication in the kitchen, and the last 100 pages of the book contain many of Jones' favorite recipes.

Booklist, December 15, 2007

among the literati. He is someone, in other words, whose latest work needs looking at and commenting on in the review media—even negatively, as Kirn does in his review. The heading of the review immediately indicates the direction in which Kirn is headed: "Serious Trouble: John Barth Returns—Not for the Better."

And this is the review's opening paragraph:

> No, the serious novel isn't dead, but there are times when one wishes it were, if only to get the whole pretentious business over with. The publication of John Barth's *Coming Soon!!!* is such an occasion.[3]

Kirn then proceeds to summarize as best he can the novel's confusing plot—his honesty in this regard is quite refreshing—and in this castigating statement puts a bead on the nature of the story Barth is trying to tell:

> *Coming Soon!!!* is exactly as I've described it, only more off-putting and convoluted: a punning, preening puzzle of a "narrative" (that's what its publishers call the thing, at least) that, to adapt Truman Capote's famous dismissal of Jack Kerouac's *On the Road,* is not so much written as word processed.[4]

At this point in the review, Kirn places Barth's novel in a context that further develops the reasons for his negative reactions to it, summarized in these two lines:

> Thus does literature bid good riddance to its audience and go off along in a corner to sniff its fingers and doodle on the walls. . . . Rarely has language strayed as far from speech.[5]

Kirn calls seriously into question the novel's accountability, but he posits that a few readers *will* attempt to read it, under the belief that "No pain, no gain."[6]

He concludes with not only why this novel fails but also how it epitomizes Barth's whole career, which, obviously, Kirn has no great regard for, and this conclusion is the important point his review is making:

> The best books, once, were the ones you couldn't put down; the elite novels now are the ones you can't pick up. . . . Dare not to read it, then dare not to pretend to have. The world, I assure you, will be a happier place.[7]

So, the question is, does reviewing John Barth so negatively serve a purpose? The answer cannot be anything but yes. Barth has been a prominent figure in more-or-less experimental fiction for, as Kirn points out, several decades, and review attention thus needs to be given to any new work he writes. And the benefit, too, of Kirn's review is to hear what an established, reputable critic has to say about the state of today's serious, literary fiction.

PREPUBLICATION REVIEWS

Finally, what about the prepublication review media used by librarians and booksellers to select materials to carry either in their libraries or their bookstores? As noted previously, the prepublication review media include *Booklist, Library Journal,* and *Publishers Weekly.*

Reviews in these sources often provide information and opinions keyed to their library and bookstore readership. This may include identifying a specific audience for a particular book or nonprint item: for instance, readers interested in following, in close detail—undaunted by close details, that is—current events. Or this special information may connect readers fond of a certain novelist with another novelist working with similar themes and subjects and even settings. This is called "readers' advisory" in the world of librarianship, and a good librarian appreciates any trustworthy suggestions on connecting readers who have read and enjoyed, say, the historical novels of Madison Smartt Bell that deal with the political and social upheavals in early nineteenth-century Haiti, *All Souls' Rising* (1995) and *Master of the Crossroads* (2000), with the powerhouse of a historical novel by Mario Vargas Llosa, *The Feast of the Goat* (2001), which is about the 1961 assassination of Rafael Trujillo, notorious strongman of Haiti's neighbor, the Dominican Republic.

Or a review in the prepublication review sources may advise librarians on how to use the information contained in a certain book or audiobook; for instance, a science source that explains its topic in reliable, succinct terms may be used by high-school students making reports for their science class. Or a new, fresh, totally professional biography of Confederate president Jefferson Davis would be important in ensuring a library's Civil War collection is complete and comprehensive.

Good reviews are good for several reasons, and even in short space they reveal a lot of things not only about the book under review but also the reviewer. Even a short review is personal to some degree. Be mindful, then, that you are giving something of yourself away in a review!

NOTES

1. Brad Hooper, review of *Cars: A Celebration,* by Quentin Willson, *Booklist* 98 (September 15, 2001): 173.

2. Erica Wagner, "Expatriate Game," review of *Lulu in Marrakech,* by Diane Johnson, *New York Times Book Review* (October 26, 2008): 8.

3. Walter Kirn, "Serious Trouble: John Barth Returns—Not for the Better," review of *Coming Soon!!!* by John Barth, *GQ* (November 2001): 204.

4. Ibid.

5. Ibid.

6. Ibid.

7. Ibid.

WHAT MAKES A GOOD REVIEWER? 6

S uccessful real-estate agents swear by the adage that the three most important factors in guaranteeing a sale are *location, location, location,* and, as noted, this concept could be well adapted to book reviewing: the three most important factors in becoming a successful reviewer are *experience, experience, experience.*

First, *experience* reading books or listening to audiobooks; second, *experience* reading reviews; and finally, *experience* writing reviews. Generally, the individual who has an interest in writing reviews is usually referred to as a "book person." (That tagging can be taken either flatteringly or disparagingly, depending on how one senses the labeler's attitude toward someone who spends considerable time with his or her nose in a book.)

To become a good reviewer, the book person must learn to read books and listen to audiobooks critically and not simply for enjoyment. In fact, reading critically is often accomplished at the expense of a certain degree of the sheer enjoyment of reading or listening.

This point cannot be expressed too emphatically: a person interested in reviewing needs to read, read, and read (or listen) critically before beginning to think about writing reviews.

At the same time, while you are involved in your program of critical reading, you should also be reading reviews. And read even *more* reviews. Try reading a new book (or listening to an audiobook) that you know is making a splash. Save all the reviews you see written about it, but do not read the reviews until you have finished reading (or listening to) the book. Then compare your reactions to the reactions of the reviewer.

Or vice versa: read all the reviews you can about a new book, and keeping them close at hand, now read the book, all the while searching out all the points the reviewers have made. (This will result in a not particularly *smooth* read, but think of it as an anatomy course; you have the textbook in hand as you dissect the body, and it helps you to identify each organ and gland. And in our case, you use the reviews to dissect the book as you read it.)

Just as dissection of the human body is an absolutely necessary requisite in a medical education, dissection of books or audiobooks is absolutely necessary for an education in reviewing. As indicated previously, it will not be the same reading or listening experience as before. You cannot simply sit back and enjoy. You must constantly analyze, forever dissecting the book or audiobook and identifying its component parts.

GETTING STARTED

You do not want to disassemble a book? You want only to enjoy it—in its wholeness and completeness—or just learn from it, if it is an educational book? Then don't be a reviewer, as simple as that. It is your choice.

But for those who seriously want to review, there comes a point when you have been reading critically for some time, and you have been reading all the reviews you can get your hands on (and using them to help analyze the works you have been reading or listening to); and now it is time to try your hand at writing reviews. (Chapter 7 lists several nonfiction and fiction titles as possible candidates to read and review.)

The Short Review

Start with a short review, about 175 words. You will be surprised at how necessary it is to practice concision when facing a 175-word limit. It certainly is not easy to express yourself about a book or audiobook in 175 words, because you have to remember that, even in a short review, you must answer both of the crucial questions that always must be answered in a review: What is the book (or audiobook) about? How good is it?

If you find you do not have 175 words to say about the item you are reviewing, then perhaps you should try another book or audiobook. If the second time you still can't come up with 175 words for a review, then it would be wise to reconsider whether reviewing is really an endeavor you should pursue.

The Full-Length Review

After you have practiced the art of concision in several 175-word reviews, then allow yourself—or compel yourself, as the case may be—to go "full length": 500 words, the average length of a feature review in a newspaper review section, whether in print or online. If you are writing a 500-word review of a novel, do not simply fill the review with plot description. Remember the other elements of a fiction review, discussed in chapter 4: character, theme, setting, and style. Recall, too, that you must answer the how-good-is-it question. Five hundred words simply recapitulating for the reader that "she did this, and then she did that" will not suffice. Readers will forget two minutes after they have read your review most of the facets of the plot that you have ever-so-carefully charted for them. It is best to remember that a long retelling of the plot—a lengthy mapping of what happens next—will make a review tiresome to read and consequently make the book or audiobook sound boring even if it most definitely is *not*.

AN EXERCISE

Try this exercise: find a newish book you know is being widely reviewed, and collect various reviews of it and keep them together—but don't read them yet. First, read the book and write a mock review of it; and then read all the other reviews. What if the majority of the reviews are pointing out a strength you didn't see, or you thought was *not* a strength? Or what if most of them criticized an element of the book that simply escaped you or that you had not seen as a detriment to the book's effectiveness? Do not regard the other reviews as "correct" and yours as "wrong." Instead, reread the book and see where you then stand on what the majority of other reviews—contrary to yours—had pointed out as strengths and weaknesses. If after rereading the book, you still believe you are right, then you *are* right!

Remember, judging a book or audiobook—even by closely following the guidelines we have set down for identifying and isolating and weighing the elements of a book by which it *should* be judged—is a subjective call. It most definitely should be a well-considered call, but even an opinion based on specific evidence and clear thinking will still be just that: an *opinion*.

NO OVERWRITING ALLOWED

We have established that experience is crucial—no, *vital*—in a good reviewer. Experience reading books, experience reading reviews, and experience writing reviews.

But in addition to experience, good writing skills are absolutely necessary to be a successful reviewer. What is meant by good writing skills is not an ability to spell, or to make subject and verb agree, or to possess a good arsenal of adjectives and adverbs useful in analysis. What is meant by good writing skills is the ability to express oneself in well-wrought language that has, at once, color and flourish but without being overly wrought. Floweriness has no place, in other words.

It is not difficult for reviewers, even ones with experience under their belts, to fall into the unfortunate habit of *competing* with the book or audiobook they are reviewing. They draw attention to themselves by overwriting. It is all perfectly well and good—necessary, in fact—for a reviewer to be forthcoming in proffering answers to the questions of what the book is about and how good it is. A review is nothing if not a setting for the reviewer's answers to these questions. But sometimes reviewers unconsciously—perhaps even consciously—desire to impress the reader of the review with their *own* writerly talents, as if to insist that even though they are "only" writing a review, offering a critique of someone *else's* creativity, they have to prove, at the same time, their creativeness as well; and consequently, they draw attention to *their* writing style, as opposed to their critical skills, by overwriting. Consider the following hypothetical example:

> This breathtaking, groundbreaking, earth-shattering novel, brimming with wisdom that soars into the stratosphere and writerly talent that storms through the narrative like the fiercest typhoon, depicts a dysfunctional family whose individual and collective sufferings make the reader wince with pinpricking recognition and yelp with the poignant frustration of not being able to enter the novel's pages oneself and help direct these characters out of the miasma into which they've sunk like precious gems that have been dropped overboard and apparently lost forever.

Overwriting in a review usually takes the form of using so many big, long, uncommon words that the writing suggests the reviewer had a thesaurus handy, in which to find a more impressive but, in truth, a more obscure word for nearly every one the reviewer ordinarily would have used. Or overwriting can involve soaring metaphors whose meaning is muddied because the image the reviewer intended to create has no concrete value. Spun from thin air and purple language, the metaphor brings to the reader no graphic, resonant visualization—and that is the whole purpose of a metaphor. But if it is just fancy language with no real meaning, then it simply draws attention to itself as such: fancy but empty language. That certainly makes the reviewer look bad, especially because the reviewer's job at hand is judging someone else's writing ability.

No one can be a successful reviewer without good analytical skills in combination with good writing skills. Again, experience plays a determinant role here—in bringing good analysis to bear on reviewing books and being able to express your analytical ideas in the most effective language. Reviewers must grasp the criteria by which a book should be judged; furthermore, these skills in judgment must be practiced to be made not only sharp but also reasonable and definitely geared to the particular book or audiobook at hand, and not simply generalized commentary that could apply to most any book.

The analytical skills of the reviewer—the acumen of the reviewer in estimating the quality of a book—means very little if the reviewer's wise, judicious, and perceptive opinions are not borne on effective language. The reviewer's ability to express an idea, whether it is in answer to the question of how good the book is or even in answer to the question of what the book is about, will make the difference in the reader of the review not only understanding the reviewer's ideas but also *enjoying* the review.

In sum, good critical ideas must remain inseparable from good writing skills, and both must be practiced and practiced again.

A GENEROUS NATURE

In covering the subject of what makes a good reviewer, the word *generous* must surface in our discussion. A good reviewer is generous. By that I do not mean soft, easy, uncritical, and only too willing to applaud any book that comes down the publishing pike simply because it *is* a book. What I do mean is that the reviewer must be open-minded and munificent.

Book lovers by definition certainly hold books in high regard; they regard the very *concept* of a book as sacred. (That is the nature, of course, of being a devotee of something.) Most book lovers consider having written and published a book the most honorable, even thrilling, reward life can offer.

But a book lover needs to realize that the publication of someone's book does not automatically mean the book is good. All kinds of bad books get published, which really should come as no surprise to anyone. On the other hand, a book reviewer should never be resentful of someone getting a book published; and a good book reviewer cannot be someone who believes the whole book publishing industry is rotten, overly commercial, and has turned its back on cultural excellence—and thus every review written should take the industry to task.

HOOPER'S REVIEWS

Best European Fiction, 2010, edited by Aleksandar Hemon (Dalkey Archive, 2010)

Dalkey Archive Press inaugurates a planned series of annual anthologies of European fiction with this impressive first volume, which gathers short stories from 30 countries. Readers for whom the expression "foreign literature" means the work of Canada's Alice Munro stand to have their eyes opened wide and their reading exposure exploded as they encounter works from places such as Croatia, Bulgaria, and Macedonia (and, yes, from more familiar terrain, such as Spain, the UK, and Russia). Even tiny Liechtenstein is represented, by a correlatively tiny but pungent story, "In the Snow," about two teenage boys hiking to another town that promises great entertainment. The stories are arranged alphabetically by home country. The first, then, is from Albania, a piece called "The Country Where No One Ever Dies," a beautifully composed and marvelously entertaining expression of Albanian cultural eccentricities. Certainly not all stories are conventional in construction or easy to decipher, but every piece benefits serious fiction lovers' reading experience. The book contains an insightful preface by novelist Zadie Smith, who overviews the included stories' commonalities and differences, as well as an introduction by Bosnian writer and volume editor Hemon, author of the highly acclaimed novel *The Lazarus Project* (2008) and now a Chicago resident, who eloquently insists that the short story is hardly a moribund literary form.

Booklist, December 1, 2009

BE CRITICAL, NOT CRABBY

Personal taste, as noted, naturally plays a part in the way a reviewer looks at a book or audiobook. That's an absolute given in reviewing. But the personal issues of the reviewer should *not* be a part of the review. A review is no place for a reviewer to grind axes about his or her personal opinions on the book industry, on the author's personality or reputation (other than critical reputation, which is fair game for discussion or even just mention in a review), or even on the subject matter at hand. Be accepting of what people want to write about and how they chose to write about it. The good reviewer will always remind himself of this.

When it comes to subject matter, reviewers simply cannot be mean in their outlook on what kind of books should and should not be published. Not simply subject matter in nonfiction but also subject matter in fiction. If a reviewer realizes that a book's subject is not one that he or she feels comfortable reading about, then the book should be given up and allowed to be reviewed by someone for whom the subject matter presents no problem.

The following comment (purely made up, by me) illustrates what I am talking about:

> This book is about aristocratic life in France in the century prior to the Revolution. A book about this time and place should be an examination of the peasantry and lower classes in the cities rather than a visit to the frivolous upper class and the ridiculous life at the royal court.

It is simply unfair to criticize a book on the basis of it being about something you are not interested in—or feel distressful about because it hits too close to home. If the subject of abortion, for instance, makes you uncomfortable or angry, then never should you review a book on the subject; if novels that deal deeply and authoritatively with family dysfunction make you break out in a cold sweat of recognition and resentment, and you simply cannot bear the truth the novel presents, you shouldn't review the book, because you are not going to be fair in judging it.

If science does not interest you, do not review a book on science. If domestic fiction bores you, do not review domestic fiction. *You cannot fault a book for what it is about.* Never forget that. Conversely, a potential reviewer should not be a prima donna and turn down books that don't exactly fit into his or her tight parameters of a "reviewing field."

Reviewers must read and learn and expand not only their reviewing but also their knowledge and worldview.

A good reviewer has to strike a balance between being too detached from what he or she is reviewing and getting too wrapped up in it. If a reviewer should never slam a book simply based on subject matter, then never should a reviewer praise a book based solely on the same basis; for example, although historical novels may be your forte, not all historical novels are good simply because they *are* historical novels. By the same token, a book advocating a liberal or a conservative social and economic agenda is not necessarily good simply because you agree with the author's political stance.

Finally, a good reviewer is able to at once stand back and see the whole forest and stand up close to observe the individual trees. But note that never does a good reviewer lose sight of the first view—the whole forest, that is—while he or she is making observations about the individual trees. The good reviewer should not get so entangled in sharing the details of a book, even if the review is to be a long one (500 words, say), that he or she does not stand back and give impressions of the book as a whole.

A few years ago, I was accepted into the Prague Summer Writers' Workshop, one of ten fortunate writers selected to study fiction writing with the esteemed novelist and short-story writer Jayne Anne Phillips. Phillips followed the traditional workshop format, each session focusing on two pieces by two workshop participants. As each piece came up for discussion, she would ask the group for general comments, and we would discuss the piece as a whole—its workability in its entirety. Then Phillips would say to the group, "Now let's go into the prose," and we would then offer our comments on the piece as we analyzed it line by line.

This workshop was a life-altering experience for me, and the lessons learned there apply to reviewing as well. Analyze the trees in a review but always be mindful of the nature of the forest as a whole, for, ultimately, the impact of the forest as a whole is more important than the plusses and minuses of each individual tree. Of course, one amounts to the other; the quality of the individual trees amounts to the quality of the forest as a whole. But *in a review,* even in a lengthy one, no matter how much a reviewer discusses the components and features of a book, the reviewer must always be mindful of not letting the readers of the review forget the contours and depth of the book as a whole.

CAVEATS

Let me end with a few warnings.
Read this sentence:

> This well-written account of the author's adventures in the Amazon is a very readable example of travel literature.

Do not use the phrase *well-written* in a review. It is nonspecific and can mean any number of things to different readers: a good writing style, or good character building, or good plot structuring. Be specific rather than leaving it to *well-written*.

HOOPER'S REVIEWS

For the Thrill of It: Leopold, Loeb, and the Murder That Shocked Chicago, by Simon Baatz (HarperCollins, 2008)

Nathan Leopold and Richard Loeb have been the objects of derision and curiosity ever since the sensational murder they committed on Chicago's South Side in 1924. These two privileged teenagers, who killed little Bobby Franks, a neighbor, also from a privileged family, just for the thrill of achieving the perfect crime ("a murder that would never be solved"), have become almost legendary "bad boys." Baatz's comprehensive account of the case succeeds in identifying their peculiar personality traits as well as what it was in the nature of their relationship that made them believe in their infallibility in performing the ultimate crime. All of Leopold and Loeb's intense planning quickly unraveled, however, when the victim's body was discovered soon after the murder; the murderers had counted on the body never being located. The second strong point of this exhaustively researched and rivetingly presented account is the thoroughness with which the author reconstructs the police investigation and the trial itself; a vivid portrait of the famous lawyer Clarence Darrow, who defended Leopold and Loeb, is a fascinating by-product. One of the best true-crime books of this or any other season.

Booklist, June 1, 2008

And the same with *readable*. What exactly does that mean? *Readable* could mean that the type font is easy on the eye. Do you mean *compelling*? Then say *compelling*.

And read this:

> The author spends the month of October 2001 on a walking tour of the Dordogne Valley in southwest France. He arrives at the town of Sarlat by train from Paris, and then he meets up with a group led by a man who is a professional tour leader. For the next ten days, the group walks from one exquisite village to another, and they eat one spectacular dinner after another.

What is wrong? Narrative nonfiction should generally be reviewed in the past tense; it actually *did* happen, but it happened only once, and it happened in the past:

> The author spent the month of October 2001 on a walking tour of the Dordogne Valley in southwest France. He arrived at the town of Sarlat by train from Paris, and then he met up with a group led by a man who was a professional tour leader. For the next ten days, the group walked from one exquisite village to another, and they ate one spectacular dinner after another.

Review fiction in the present tense, for it never actually happened, but it does happen again and again, every time the book is opened and read.

REVIEW-WRITING WORKSHOPS 7

In one of their most important capacities, in addition to being a book depository and information purveyor, public libraries host public programs. One such public program can be sponsoring review-writing workshops.

But before we begin the public-service aspect of review-writing workshops, let's focus within the library walls on review-writing services for public-library staff.

As discussed in the introduction, many librarians have a personal stake in reviewing, either because it is a component of their job descriptions or because they have freelance interests. Certainly, most libraries would not be interested in conducting review-writing programs exclusively to foster staff members' outside writing careers. But that does not preclude librarians conducting such programs to educate staff on review writing for such library-marketing strategies as announcing new arrivals in the library's collection on the library's website and preparing readers' advisory handouts, among others. Such a program could well be open to staff members who are interested in review writing *only* to help satisfy their own personal freelance needs.

How to conduct a review-writing program? Think of such a program in terms of a workshop with audience participation, and not simply a presentation in lecture format.

First of all, line up someone to conduct the workshop: a local writer with review-writing experience or, in the absence of such a person in your community, a staff member in your library who has the most review-writing experience to his or her credit.

The next step would be, particularly if the program leader has limited review-writing experience, for the leader to study this book and get comfortable with its ideas on reviewing.

Next, post an announcement about the workshop for the staff and, if so desired, the public, and give the workshop coordinator plenty of time to prepare. Around 10 days before the event, writing-workshop participants must submit to the on-site workshop coordinator a 175-word "mock" review they have written about a new book or audiobook that has caught their attention. The workshop director then will make copies of all the participants' reviews and pass copies of every review to the participants with the instruction to be prepared to discuss the reviews during the workshop. Remember, reviews should be submitted to the coordinator anonymously, and copies are passed out to participants anonymously.

The workshop, after opening comments, should begin with the leader describing the elements of reviewing and the characteristics of good reviewers as laid out in this book and added to or improvised by the workshop leader based on his or her own concepts of reviewing.

Then the discussions begin; the author of the piece under discussion remains unknown, so the review writers have no need to "defend" or explain their composition. In other words, they must sit quietly and take it—the good and the bad.

The workshop works best with approximately a dozen participants. This limited number keeps the time frame under control and allows every review to be fully discussed. If many people sign up, two or even three workshops could be held over as many days, so that all interested individuals can be accommodated. Much fewer than a dozen participants sometimes results in participants' awkwardness in airing views and opinions—but sometimes the smaller number has the opposite effect: participants may open up easier than in front of a dozen people.

The workshop leader must stay flexible and be sensitive to the mood of the group, and if the leader senses that participants are being shy, it is up to the leader to ease the atmosphere in the room and coax people to open up and talk. This is best done by showing the group, from the very first, that nothing the participants say will be put down as wrong.

The workshop leader can also give every participant a "workshop evaluation" form, to be filled out at the end and turned in to the leader. The form should be direct and uncomplicated, with just three elements:

What part of the workshop was most helpful? What part of the workshop was least helpful? Rate the overall effectiveness of the workshop on a scale of one to ten.

The workshop leader can use the results of the evaluation form to possibly improve the presentation and to promote the workshop to other librarians.

WRITING MOCK REVIEWS

In chapter 6, I shared an exercise for beginning reviewers to gain reviewing experience by writing mock reviews (of actual current books) and then comparing these reviews with other—*actual*—reviews of the same title. To aid in that exercise—in case you are awash in possibilities for writing mock reviews and don't know where to turn—I offer the following selections as highly recommended candidates.

The method to my madness is this: the range is wide, covering several nonfiction subject areas and types of fiction, and I have selected titles of which you can find reviews on Amazon.com. The philosophy behind my selection is to encourage new reviewers, learner reviewers, to broaden and strengthen their newly developing reviewing muscle by reviewing beyond their exclusive personal interests and reviewing against customary gender interests:

> A watercolor book for the nonartist
>
> A short-story collection for readers who believe they can enjoy only novels
>
> A Civil War history for women who assume that subject is only a male interest
>
> A romance for men delving for the first time into romance fiction
>
> A crime novel for women newly entering the world of hard-boiled detective fiction
>
> A nonfiction book about a famous women's shoe company to be read by men
>
> Literary fiction for readers usually comfortable only with popular novels

A travel book for someone who appreciates *not* leaving home

And finally, as a reward to hardworking readers, a biography for readers who know they love biographies

All titles I present are suitable for reviewing by general readers. For each title, I give the briefest of identifier; yes, I don't want to hand you too much material to use in writing your reviews. And here they are:

Understanding Color: Creative Techniques in Watercolor, by Marcia Moses (Sterling). For beginners eager to try their hand at a venerable medium.

How It Ended: New and Collected Stories, by Jay McInerny (Knopf). From the author of the novel *Bright Lights, Big City* (1985), proof that the author is also a splendid short-story writer.

Team of Rivals: The Political Genius of Abraham Lincoln, by Doris Kearns Goodwin (Simon and Schuster). This collective biography highlights the men who were Lincoln's rivals for the presidency but whom he brought into his cabinet for a powerful working force.

All of Me, by Lori Wilde (Forever). This is the fourth installment in the author's popular Wedding Veil Wishes series of romance novels.

Rough Weather, by Robert B. Parker (Putnam). The thirty-sixth Spenser novel involves kidnapping as well as murder.

The Towering World of Jimmy Choo: A Glamorous Story of Power, Profits, and the Pursuit of the Perfect Shoe, by Lauren Goldstein Crowe (Bloomsbury). The history of the ups and downs of the Jimmy Choo shoe brand.

People of the Book, by Geraldine Brooks (Penguin). A fictionalized history of a book—a Hebrew codex known as the Sarajevo Haggadah.

Ghost Train to the Eastern Star: On the Tracks of the Great Railway Bazaar, by Paul Theroux (Houghton Mifflin). The famous travel writer retraces his steps as first chronicled in *The Great Railway Bazaar.*

Flannery: A Life of Flannery O'Connor, by Brad Gooch (Little, Brown). The life and career of an eminent southern fiction writer.

RELEVANT WEBSITES

What follows is a listing of a handful of articles and relevant websites of interest to new reviewers.

"Tips for Successful Book Reviewing," by the National Book Critics Circle, the name of the group self-explanatory as to who belongs. The subtitle of the document is "Strategies for Breaking In and Staying In." This is, obviously, words from the professionals. The site is http://bookcritics.org/articles/archive/tips_for_successful_book_reviewing.

"How to Write a Decent Book Review" is the title of an online document that has been prepared by GraceAnne DeCandido, former editor of *Wilson Library Bulletin* and reviewer for many years for *Booklist, Library Journal,* and *Kirkus.* She shares a succinct listing of her thoughts on what she has learned about reviewing during her long career. This page can be reached at www.well.com/user/ladyhawk/bookrevs .html.

Visit http://papercuts.blogs.nytimes.com/2008/03/25/seven-deadly -words-of-book-reviewing to be both educated and amused by an article called "Seven Deadly Words of Book Reviewing," written by Bob Harris, in which he provocatively cites seven words that are used so often in reviews that they have become reviewing clichés, including such surprising choices as *poignant* and more obvious ones, such as *eschew.*

"How to Write a Book Review" comes from Los Angeles Valley College Library (www.lacv.cc.cn.us/Library/bookreview.htm). The rundown on "standard procedures for writing book reviews" is an excellent brief course on the subject.

WRITING AUDIOBOOK REVIEWS 8

Joyce Saricks

Surely reviews are reviews—what makes audiobook reviews different? There is an easy answer: the narrator. However, that may be the only easy part! Describing the role of the narrator and what the narrator brings to the listener's experience of the book is a tough job for reviewers. With books, we can talk about how the author uses language, symbolism, and characters to tell his story. With audio, we must acknowledge what the narrator adds with just the voice to enhance our appreciation of the story.

This being the case, the vital point to remember in reviewing audiobooks is that the focus of the review is the narrator and the narration, not the story. By the time the audio review is published, most readers have read about the book and they know the basic story. They need to know how the audio enriches our experience of the story or the issues that make this a less-than-stellar experience.

LISTENING AND COMPILING NOTES

The reviewing process begins by listening to the audiobook. Unless your recall is perfect, that means taking notes as well. I try to write down impressions. How does the narration strike me? Does the voice work for the characters and for the book in terms of accents and general tone? Can I identify ways that the listening experience enriches the book? I confess it is hard not to get involved in plot twists, and those observations can be useful—whether the narrator makes the story easy to follow or not—but more important is how the narrator uses her voice to bring this story to life in our imagination. Identifying these factors is not easy, but if we are conscious of our mission as we listen, it is often easier to catch aspects worth sharing.

It is helpful to consider the appeal of the narration in the same way we think about the appeal of books—language and style, tone and mood, pacing, characterization, story line, background frame, and setting. This is not all that hard, because we naturally describe books using these adjectives that allow us to express how a book has affected us. Not all the elements play a role in every book we read or listen to, but thinking in terms of appeal helps us focus and consolidate our thoughts.

Language and Style

Language may be the first element we recognize—and relate to. Does the narrator accurately pronounce personal names, geographic places, foreign words? Mispronunciations are one of the surest ways to pull readers out of the story and break the narrator's spell. If he is not saying this word correctly, can we trust him with other words with which we may not be familiar? Accents are crucial in establishing characters. Does the narrator correctly reflect speech patterns and pronunciations from a particular geographic area? Often foreign words and phrases are delivered in such a way that we understand them immediately. Books filled with dialect are almost always easier to understand heard than read. (In fact, listeners may not even realize that the written word might not be familiar, because when heard, the words are instantly understandable.) If there is dialect, it should sound right.

Cadence is also essential. Some authors are known for the particular cadence or rhythm of the speech patterns in their novels. Elmore Leonard and Robert B. Parker write with unique rhythms that come alive when read effectively. Many classics—*The Odyssey* and *The Iliad* for example—were made to be heard. Cadence is the rhythm that makes the words sing.

Tone and Mood

Audiobooks excel in conveying tone and mood. The narrator's voice sets the stage for the story, similarly to a movie soundtrack. Comic, serious, building sexual tension or suspense—the mood of the book should be reflected in the narrator's voice. Can you hear the humor in the witty repartee in a romance? Do you feel the character's dread as the suspense builds? Is the mood mystical or mysterious, playful or edgy, thoughtful or lighthearted, dark or optimistic? The narrator's voice effectively dramatizes the mood and places the listener in the story.

Pacing

When we read, we often do not notice the pacing, although we likely have an impression of whether the book reads quickly or slowly. With audio, we lose our ability to skim, and because the narrator speaks every word, she has complete control of the pace of the books. Does the narrator read too quickly or too slowly? (If the listener is aware of pace, perhaps sensing the narrator reads too quickly or slowly, there may be a problem.) When the suspense ratchets up, does the narrator move the story quickly enough? Or does the narrator savor the lovely, evocative language without allowing the story to drag? Does the snappy dialogue really sizzle? As listeners, are we as caught up in the pace of a book as we would be as readers?

Characterization

Characterization is vital for many listeners, and many narrators pride themselves on their interpretative abilities as well as their skills with unique voices and accents. Does the narrator distinguish among characters, establish them through dialects, accents, tone, pitch? Are there linguistic quirks that make characters engaging or detestable? Are accents and pitch used accurately and appropriately? If the author allows us glimpses into the minds of the characters, does the narrator present these effectively? Are the characters portrayed consistently throughout, with voices aged through the story if appropriate?

Story Line

The audio version of a book should convey the story line accurately. Sometimes the oral version has a greater impact, because the narrator uses inflection and emphasis to stress sections we might read over too quickly. Does the reader enhance or detract from the story? Does he provide proper emphasis to themes or undercut the author's purpose? If the plot is complex and filled with multiple story lines and characters, can we follow the action and keep everyone straight? Sometimes the narrator absolutely disappears into the story. We are not aware of the voice in particular, just of the story being told us. And sometimes that approach works perfectly for the book.

Background Frame and Setting

Background frame and setting are trickier. Many popular titles today have story lines in both the past and the present, with the past providing a background for the story. In novels such as Geraldine Brooks's *People of the Book*, the story frequently flips from present to past, and the narrator is required to lead the listener through these transitions with only verbal cues about the time period.[1] How well does the narrator handle these background passages? Do we get bogged down in the details, or does her enthusiasm make us want to know more?

Is audio a good choice for this book? Titles with maps, illustrations, footnotes, and so forth, do not always translate well into audio, although excellent narrators can overcome many of these potential problems. For example, in *The Curious Incident of the Dog in the Night-Time*, by Mark Haddon, Jeff Woodman describes the hero's drawings with such precision that listeners likely will not feel they have missed anything.[2]

Finally, consider the appeal of the voice itself. Is it appropriate for the book or a mismatch? What about the tone? It might be warm (to narrate a romance or to voice the hero and heroine in any genre), cold or hard (for the villain or for any dangerous character or situation), distant (to make us observers, voyeurs, in psychological suspense titles by authors such as Ruth Rendell), or intimate, menacing, melancholy, or disturbing.

Recognizing these factors and then figuring out how to express them can be tricky. But the more we think about these as we listen, and the more we struggle to express them, the easier the process becomes. (Thinking this way as we listen and practicing talking about the audio experience in these terms make us more effective working with patrons, whether we write reviews or not!)

WRITING THE REVIEW

Writing the review, we pull together our notes from listening and think beyond what we have jotted down to the best way to describe this experience. We can talk about the relentless pace or the easy flow of the story. The layered story line or plot twists that keep us in the car in the driveway just to hear what happens next. The sense that we know these characters and can relate to their plight—or the haunting feeling that things are not quite right here. Good narrators intensify our experience of the story, and how they do that is precisely the information we want to share in our review.

Although less is more with plot description, a sentence or two that establishes the plot and the characters sets up the review. You may want to start with plot, or you may want to start with an impression related to the narrator or narration. In his review of Jeffery Deaver's chilling *The Bodies Left Behind,* David Pitt hooks us with this sentence: "Deaver, the master of plot twists, hits another one out of the park with this story of a Michigan police deputy whose investigation of a suspicious 911 call leads to danger as she soon finds herself being chased through the woods by two killers."[3] He manages to establish the popularity of the author, a quick sense of the plotline, and the mood, all in one sentence.

In contrast, Mary McCay emphasizes the narration in the opening sentences of her review of the recording of Richard Yates's *Revolutionary Road.* "Yates' 1961 novel chronicles 'the hopeless emptiness of everything in this country.' And that emptiness and other emotions are rendered both real and frighteningly current through Bramhall's reading, which is both meticulously paced and individually toned to each set of characters."[4] She then goes on to provide a quick plot summary, but she has established the excellence of the narration with this introduction.

While listening, we look for the appeal elements listed above. Incorporating them into the review helps our audience identify them as well. In fact, this is something we do automatically as we reflect on the importance of the narration. Although I describe each of these elements separately, it is clear that they overlap and that comments may cover more than one element. The point is, of course, to convey the narrator's skill to the review reader, whether by focusing on a single point or covering several elements in a descriptive phrase or sentence.

Take language, for example. In her review of Elmore Leonard's *Mr. Paradise,* Karen Harris writes, "[Narrator] Forster combines an uncanny ability to delineate the various characters through his streetwise, cynical, and sardonic vocal intonations; perfect timing; and appropriate inflection. He perfectly conveys Leonard's unique humor and dialogue."[5]

In just two sentences, she addresses Leonard's distinctive dialogue and cadence, important points for any listener familiar with his work.

Accents, dialect, and diverse characters provide a grand stage for skilled narrators. In Marion James's *The Book of Night Women*, Candace Smith praises narrator Robin Miles. "James' prose is more poetry than narrative, and Miles' Caribbean cadence flows along the story line. . . . Other conspiring slaves are distinguished through changes in pace, speech patterns, and accents."[6] On the other hand, a reading without accents can be equally effective. In his performance of Pearl S. Buck's *The Good Earth*, narrator Anthony Heald does not attempt a Chinese accent. Neal Wyatt writes that "he softly eases into tonal shifts, adding hints of an accent that are hard to pin down but lovely to hear. His wise decision not to force a false sound into his reading allows listeners to fully enjoy and luxuriate in the lovely cadence of the narration."[7] Both methods—using accents or not—can be effective, and both should always be acknowledged in the review.

Mood and tone come across clearly in audiobooks. Take humor, for example. Simon Prebble excels at evoking this mood in his reading of Julia Quinn's witty Regency romances. An excerpt from my review of *It's in His Kiss* highlights this skill. "Prebble's virtuoso performance provides the perfect combination of urbane and seductive tones, capturing the emotional intensity and range—from humor to passion—of this high-spirited romance. With tongue firmly in cheek, he intones the lengthy and humorous chapter headings; listeners hear the laughter in his voice and are powerless to resist. His clear diction and careful emphasis highlight the delightful repartee, a hallmark of Quinn's style."[8] Surely that is enough information to decide whether such a title would please your patrons and useful information to share with a potential listener. However, humor is likely easier than the sense of menace that accompanies suspense and thrillers or the more thoughtful tone of many literary titles. Mary Frances Wilkens considers Maggie-Meg Reed's narration of Lisa Gardner's thriller *Hide*. Her "poised narration balances the frenetic action and tension, making it hard to turn off the audio in anticipation of what might happen next."[9] Just the mood readers expect!

Pacing, as I suggested above, may be whether the narrator reads at an appropriate speed for the action or description. It is also tied to the cadence. An excellent example is Lisette Lecat's narration of Alexander McCall Smith's No. 1 Ladies' Detective Agency series. In her review of *The Miracle at Speedy Motors,* Alison Block comments that Lecat "renders the lively lilt and cadence of the Botswanan characters. . . . Her perfect reading pace enables listeners to savor the morsels of wisdom spread throughout the tale."[10] Her reading pace sets the stage for the leisurely unfolding mystery and underlines the charm of the series.

Characterization is more straightforward. We need to be able to distinguish who is speaking, whether narrators assume particular voices or reflect characters through changes in pitch and accent. However, the best reviews reveal nuances. Laurie Hartshorn identifies the "touch of oiliness" Richard Poe brings to the role of the usurping uncle in David Wroblewski's *The Story of Edgar Sawtelle.* More complicated to portray, however, is the character of Edgar, who is mute. "When Edgar is signing, Poe uses a flat, breathy inflection that seems just right for the intelligent boy, who has lots of thoughts but no spoken words."[11]

The narration can also affect our perception of the story. Sissy Spacek's interpretation of *To Kill a Mockingbird* offers an interesting style. Many know the story line and characters primarily from the 1962 film with Gregory Peck, but the novel is written from young Scout's point of view, and Spacek chose not to differentiate among the characters but to tell it all in the young girl's voice. In her review of the audiobook, Neal Wyatt wrote, "The characters are larger than life, but actor Spacek, with her amazing narration, wipes all of that away, leaving only her voice behind."[12]

Although many popular titles today use flashbacks, which require the narrator to switch fluidly between time periods as well as characters, other novels and nonfiction present even more complex issues. In Susanna Clarke's award-winning *Jonathan Strange and Mr. Norrell,* consummate narrator Simon Prebble must contend not only with a complex plot and myriad characters (each with a distinct, recognizable voice) but he must also seamlessly incorporate lengthy footnotes, vital to the story, leaving the listener with no doubt about what is footnote and what is story.

Audiobook reviewers might also provide an overall impression of the narration and how well it reflects the author's style and intent. In her review of Terry Pratchett's young adult title *Nation,* Mary Burkey writes, "Briggs' eloquent reading, with perfectly balanced expression, begins with restrained tones that intensify listener's engagement. . . . [Briggs] infuses his speech with the rhythm of the author's wry British wit, shifting from laugh-out-loud humor to pure sentiment with complete unaffectedness."[13]

Another factor to consider is who the narrator is. Has she read other titles by this author or in this series? Is he an experienced, award-winning narrator or a new voice? Because audiobook fans often follow narrators, it is good to remind selectors that a narrator likely has a following. And because the narrator's role is so important, any exceptional performance should be noted, as libraries will likely want to add the title to the collection whether the author is known or not. Does the author read his own work? Is he successful? Memoirs narrated by the authors are often more heartfelt and engaging, because the author is telling her own stories. On the other hand, novels or narrative nonfiction titles may honestly be beyond an author's narrative skill. This is not a reason to pan a recording or to discourage libraries from purchasing, but the author's skill as narrator should be noted.

Of course, reviewers must also check the spelling of names of characters and places if they are used in the review. Unfortunately, the package almost never contains everything you need to know and want to include. You may need to go to the book to do this, as it is all too easy to confuse Elinor and Eleanor, John and Jon, and so many more. Include the series name too, if the title is part of a series.

Are there extra features? Music at the beginning and end of disks or at appropriate intervals throughout that intensifies the mood? Sound effects? A cast list for productions with multiple narrators? Until recently, the packaging and publishing material was irritatingly obscure about who read what character. Thankfully, that seems to be changing. Certainly, it is better in a review to name narrators and their characters rather than having to guess who read what.

Remember too that profanity, sex, and violence are intensified in audio, because they come directly into our ears and understanding. Skimming is not as easy when we listen, so a word of warning about particularly explicit sections may be useful. Observing this likely will not stop someone from purchasing, but it can be invaluable information when talking with potential listeners.

Do not be afraid to list listen-alikes—that is, other books that hold a similar appeal—in the review. If we are matching author to author, these may be similar to those we would offer readers. It is helpful, however, to take the narrator and the listening experience into account as well. As we listened, of what other authors and titles did this remind us? What narrators can create similar moods?

As in all reviewing, the reviewer should remain objective. I may not personally like the story or the narrator, but that does not mean it rates a negative review. Reviewers have an obligation to provide information about the quality of the listening experience and the production, to praise what is done well, and to identify any problems. If it does not please us, we need to be specific about the problems. Poor quality recording? A voice that does not work for the story and characters? Infelicitous accents or speech patterns that do not fit the book? Is the pace or cadence off? Specifics provide the information selectors need as well as useful details for public service staff.

READING AUDIO REVIEWS

Just as we do when we read book reviews, we look for those elements that suggest the quality and appeal of the audiobook. Watch for the adjectives that describe the impact of the narration.

Certainly reviews should provide enough information for us to decide whether to purchase an audiobook or not, but they should also enhance our understanding of what a narrator brings to this production. This is information we can then share with fans of audio—to introduce them to an author or book or narrator or to introduce them to the experience of listening. Reviews can affirm our satisfaction in a narrator or introduce us to others. How many listeners who loved Harry Potter will follow narrator Jim Dale to every book he reads? Certainly enough to make buying all those titles a priority.

Even if the reviewer does not include listen-alikes, we can sometimes discover our own, just from the language that identifies the appeal of the book and narrator. What other books, authors, and listening experiences does this description bring to mind? The more we think this way, the easier it is to recognize listen-alikes and share them with readers.

Audiobook reviews explore the way a narrator, with only his voice, animates the author's characters, story, and prose. Careful listening and thoughtful consideration of the role of the narrator and the effect of the narration allow reviewers to identify the appeal of the production. Effective reviews aid collection development librarians, public service staff, and audiobook fans, as they communicate the pleasures of story heard rather than read.

NOTES

1. Geraldine Brooks, *People of the Book* (New York: Penguin Audio, 2008). Edwina Wren, narrator.

2. Mark Haddon, *The Curious Incident of the Dog in the Night-Time* (Prince Frederick, MD: Recorded Books, 2003). Jeff Woodman, narrator.

3. David Pitt, review of *The Bodies Left Behind,* by Jeffery Deaver, *Booklist* 105 (March 1, 2009): 69. Holter Graham, narrator.

4. Mary McCay, review of *Revolutionary Road,* by Richard Yates, *Booklist* 105 (April 1, 2009): 72. Mark Bramhall, narrator.

5. Karen Harris, review of *Mr. Paradise,* by Elmore Leonard, *Booklist* 100 (April 15, 2004): 1450. Robert Forster, narrator.

6. Candace Smith, review of *The Book of Night Women,* by Marion James, *Booklist* 105 (April 15, 2009): 58. Robin Miles, narrator.

7. Neal Wyatt, review of *The Good Earth,* by Pearl S. Buck, *Booklist* 104 (December 1, 2007): 65. Anthony Heald, narrator.

8. Joyce Saricks, review of *It's in His Kiss,* by Julia Quinn, *Booklist* 103 (September 15, 2006): 76. Simon Prebble, narrator.

9. Mary Frances Wilkens, review of *Hide,* by Lisa Gardner, *Booklist* 103 (May 1, 2007): 50. Maggie-Meg Reed, narrator.

10. Alison Block, review of *The Miracle at Speedy Motors,* by Alexander McCall Smith, *Booklist* 104 (August 2008): 86. Lisette Lecat, narrator.

11. Laurie Hartshorn, review of *The Story of Edgar Sawtelle,* by David Wroblewski, *Booklist* 105 (December 15, 2009): 86. Richard Poe, narrator.

12. Neal Wyatt, review of *To Kill a Mockingbird,* by Harper Lee, *Booklist* 103 (December 1, 2006): 70. Sissy Spacek, narrator.

13. Mary Burkey, review of *Nation,* by Terry Pratchett, *Booklist* 105 (February 1, 2009): 62. Stephen Briggs, narrator.

WRITING
ANNOTATIONS

A frequently asked question when I give review-writing workshops
to librarians is, What is the difference between a review and an
annotation? The answer is primarily *length*. An annotation generally runs
between twenty-five and fifty words; the good annotation, the *excellent*
annotation, will have a lot to say about a book or audiobook in those few
words.

How to select the best twenty-five to fifty words to suit the occasion?
Remember, if a review gives a taste of the book or audiobook, then an
annotation imparts just a whiff. The two major questions that must be
answered in a review—What is the item under review about? How good
is it?—are still to be answered in an annotation, just in briefer space and
thus fewer words.

Perhaps ironically, the easier of the two questions to answer in an
annotation is, How good is it? In the interest of brevity, only one modifier
in answer to that question will suffice: "The author takes an *effective* look
at . . ." or "The *well-drawn* characters . . ." In the condensation required
in an annotation, any more than one modifier, or two at most, will strike
the reader as overwriting.

The most difficult aspect of preparing an annotation is answering
the question, What is the book or audiobook about? Yet, given the word-
length limitations of the annotation, communicating the content of the
item under consideration would seem easier than doing so in a review.
Not so! And here is the reason: the requisite concision of an annotation
means that when answering this question, the annotation writer has to
be general rather than specific. And what that means is the annotation
writer must stand back to see the audiobook or book as—to employ
a familiar metaphor—a *complete forest* rather than dwelling on the

individual trees. The annotation writer must consider which aspect of the book's features needs to be brought to the fore as the best answer to the question, What is the book about?

The annotation writer has only one long sentence, or two shorter sentences, to communicate a book's point and distinctiveness.

In nonfiction, content must be identified; and treatment of that particular subject should be recognized. If it can be covered in a phrase—or two, at most—the book's helpfulness in understanding its subject and its place in library collections can also be cited.

To reiterate, *what* part of a book to highlight is the annotation writer's choice.

In an annotation, a novel needs to be anchored in setting, but it should be affixed to its time and place in very tight language. A novel needs some mention of theme, however brief is that mention. Major characters, the author's writing style, and the plot deserve attention in the annotation only if these factors are deemed primary among the novel's characteristics.

Brevity, then, rules the day in annotation writing. Very general identifiers and criticism are to be favored over detailed ones—no, not favored, but demanded. As noted, judge a book or audiobook as you would behold the forest in its entirety, not regarding the individual trees. As in review writing, this takes practice. Annotations are not easily written; selecting the exact words and deciding which peculiar quality is most prominent and the most "citable"—and thus characterizes the book most directly and meaningfully—is nearly an art. You cannot learn an art form in an evening.

MY FAVORITE
REVIEWERS

T he following—a handful of my favorite reviewers—are master reviewers whose reviews are beneficial for the budding reviewer. Like unfledged painters honing their skills by sitting before the works of the great masters in a museum gallery, and there reproducing in their sketchbook what they see, potential and new reviewers should study the following writers to see why their reviews work so well.

John Updike

The most "unavoidable" reviewer, that is, the most prominent reviewer in today's world and consequently the first reviewer that a novice reviewer should take notice of, is the late John Updike, who died in 2009. Updike reviewed primarily in the pages of the *New Yorker,* but other serial publications, such as the *New York Review of Books* and the *New York Times Book Review,* also welcomed his peerless, cultured prose. His reviews have been gathered in two monumental collections, *Hugging the Shore* (1983) and *Due Considerations* (2007).

New reviewers should read these two impressive books cover to cover, and either book can be dipped into here and there productively, for even a minute spent between their covers will enlighten the reader about not only the particular book under review but also the *qualities* of a thoroughly engaging review as practiced by Updike.

Besides Updike's rich style, where word choice and metaphor are luxurious but not showy, the most amazing characteristic of Updike as reviewer was his ecumenism. Difficult Eastern European writers passed under his benevolent eye, and his intelligence made assessing them not difficult; and his inherent lack of condescension, his disinterest in dismissiveness, permitted him to offer serious, trenchant, as well as lively commentary on, say, Doris Day's autobiographical volume. He never promoted the second-rate, but, as significantly, he never cowered before the first-rate.

Eudora Welty

My favorite short-story writer of all time (and the short story is a form I greatly appreciate and have read widely in) is Eudora Welty (1909–2001), the remarkable lady from Jackson, Mississippi, who wrote powerful—and certainly unfussy—fiction about southern life. She was genteel in her personal life, but her fiction never suffered from prissiness.

Welty was a wise and compassionate reviewer. Her reviews can be found gathered in *A Writer's Eye: Collected Book Reviews* (1994). Individually, previously, her reviews appeared primarily in the *New York Times Book Review*. Chronologically, they range throughout most of her writing career, from 1942 to 1981. The charge of obscurantism often leveled at her fiction has no place in the estimation and appreciation of her reviewing style. Her ideas and word choice are crystal clear as she reviews—again, to me, the hallmark of the true and truly good reviewer—a range of books and authors, with no hint of either overawe or snootiness.

Indeed, many of the works and authors she reviews have been long forgotten in contemporary times: for instance, *City Limit,* a novel by Hollis Summers published in 1948. Her positive appraisal concludes: "The author has compassion, a good eye not conditioned by anything, a good ear conditioned by some worthwhile anger, and a view of youth and innocence that is fresh, dignified, and rewarding."[1] Welty makes current readers, as she did contemporaneous ones, want to go secure the novel and read it.

But passing under her reviewing eye were also such lasting names as Virginia Woolf, William Faulkner, E. B. White, and E. M. Forster. The wideness—the generosity—of her reviewing ken is reflected in her deep appreciation of mystery writer Ross Macdonald ("Mr. Macdonald's writing is something like a stand of clean, cool, well-ranched, well-tended trees in which bright birds can flash and perch. And not for show, but to sing").[2] Coincidentally, Welty's collection of reviews is dedicated to Nona Balakian, my next favorite reviewer.

Nona Balakian

Nona Balakian is a figure largely forgotten now (she died in 1991), kept in the public consciousness solely by the Nona Balakian Award given every year to an outstanding book critic by the National Book Critics Circle. Literary critic Balakian was on the editorial staff of the *New York Times Sunday Book Review* and brought many prominent fiction writers on board as reviewers, including Eudora Welty, Joyce Carol Oates, and Kurt Vonnegut. She was a founding member of the National Book Critics Circle and served on Pulitzer Prize committees. Several of her reviews (most published previously in the *Sunday Book Review* but also in such other periodicals as the *New Leader, Kenyon Review,* and the *Columbia Journalism Review*) are gathered in *Critical Encounters: Literary Views and Reviews, 1953–1977* (Bobbs-Merrill, 1978).

She was a no-nonsense reviewer, getting quickly to the heart of the dual questions: What is the book about? How good is it? As a reviewer, she is both stately and trenchant; at heart, as anyone who reads her can tell, she simply loved books.

Walter Kirn

Another favorite reviewer of mine—a controversial choice, I grant you—is Walter Kirn. Kirn is also a fiction writer, and his novels (five in total so far) are fine but not excellent. It is in his reviewing that his mind and writerly talent shine. (I believe that, ultimately, in the long run, he will be remembered more for his reviewing than his fiction writing.)

He used to be the literary editor at *GQ* magazine, where he continues to be, along with the same service for *Time* magazine, a contributing editor. He reviews regularly for the *New York Times Book Review.* You have encountered him in chapter 2 of my book, where he reviewed Rick Moody's *Demonology,* and also in chapter 5, in my discussion of negative reviewing, where he reviewed John Barth's novel *Coming Soon!!!* and strongly disapproved of it.

The latter review is a prime example of Kirn's reviewing: not necessarily negative but certainly spunky. He is the sort of guy who pulls no punches—extremely articulate and decidedly opinionated. No Gentle Ben is he, but that is a good thing; he stirs things up, keeps writers and readers on their toes. I like him, not only because of his engaging writing style and unique perceptions but also because even if he does not make you want to read the book, you have had a provocative journey though his review.

Michiko Kakutani

Negativity in reviewing brings to mind Michiko Kakutani. I discuss her here not because she is a favorite of mine in the usual sense. In other words, no warmth do I feel for her work. In fact, I often disapprove of her reviewing sense, and I'm not alone in that.

Kakutani has been a book reviewer for the *New York Times* since 1983. She is, in my estimation, overly critical to the point of meanness, and I often fail to see the source of her harshness in her reviews in terms of reasons to be so critical other than simply an urge to be mean. She has certain writers she will *never* like; her most famous response from an author she has placed in that category was from Norman Mailer, who insisted Kakutani is too feared at the *New York Times* to be reined in.

HOOPER'S REVIEWS

Due Considerations: Essays and Criticism, by John Updike (Knopf, 2007)

Updike is one of the few remaining true men of letters, the kind of writer who is equally at home in almost all forms and formats. Following two other staggeringly incisive, broad-ranging collections of his nonfiction prose, *Odd Jobs* (1991) and *More Matter* (1999), his latest such compilation is, like its predecessors, an elegant leviathan. Books, primarily, are the raison d'être for these pieces; most are reviews, and most were previously published in Updike's favorite home-away-from-home, the *New Yorker*. As a critic, Updike has long demonstrated honesty, intelligence, judiciousness, open-mindedness, and never an ounce of superciliousness. For instance, what he writes about Margaret Atwood here is particularly perceptive (especially in his comparison of her to fellow Canadian Alice Munro), and his commentary on Michael Ondaatje's novel *The English Patient* may come as a surprise: that the movie version "elucidates the novel and was the clearer, more unified work." Other essays gathered here are of a more personal nature—that is, not geared to book reviewing or to introducing new editions of books. These essays range topically from art and architecture to the author's estimation of his own personal predilections. A lush book to be savored over a long period of time.

Booklist, August 2007

On the other hand, she won the Pulitzer Prize for Criticism in 1978. I have included her on my list not really as an example of negative reviewing and how uncomfortable I am with reviewers who seem to take, over the long haul, great pleasure in slamming; I include her because she will always get your attention, and she cannot be ignored.

Anthony Lane

Last, and the most unconventional of my choices, is Anthony Lane, who writes movie and book reviews, as well as other pieces, for the *New Yorker* (I say *unconventional* because he is known primarily as a reviewer of movies, not books). He was brought on board by Tina Brown; he is, in my estimation, Brown's most lasting contribution to that magazine from her controversial term as editor.

Lane is a reading pleasure: beautiful writing style, deeply perceptive about movies and their individual ingredients and qualities (and failures, too, of course). What does he have to do with the kind of reviewing this book is about? Nothing customarily. But his movie reviews, as every reader interested in writing book or audiobook reviews can soon observe, perform the same task we have been discussing here in this book: answering the two questions of What is it about? and How good is it? His various approaches to answering these two questions are very instructive for the novice reviewer to observe and study, even when his answers are specifically geared to movies.

Lane's reviews and essays are gathered in *Nobody's Perfect* (2002).

NOTES

1. Eudora Welty, *A Writer's Eye: Collected Book Reviews* (Jackson, MS: University Press of Mississippi, 1994), 86.

2. Ibid., 162.

BIBLIOGRAPHY

Balakian, Nona. *Critical Encounters: Literary Views and Reviews, 1953–1977.* Indianapolis: Bobbs-Merrill, 1978; repr. New York: Ashod, 1991.

Block, Alison. Review of *The Miracle at Speedy Motors,* by Alexander McCall Smith, Lisette Lecat, narrator. *Booklist* 104 (August 2008): 86.

Bowen, Elizabeth. *The Heat of the Day.* New York: Penguin, 1949.

Brooks, Geraldine. *People of the Book.* Edwina Wren, narrator. New York: Penguin Audio, 2008.

Burkey, Mary. Review of *Nation,* by Terry Pratchett, Stephen Briggs, narrator. *Booklist* 105 (February 1, 2009): 62.

Carver, Raymond. *Will You Please Be Quiet, Please?* New York: Vintage, 1976.

Donaldson, Scott. "Possessions in *The Great Gatsby.*" Review of *The Great Gatsby,* by F. Scott Fitzgerald. *Southern Review* 37 (Spring 2001): 187–210.

Dowling, Brendan. Review of *The Destruction of the Inn,* by Randy Lee Eickhoff. *Booklist* 97 (March 15, 2001): 1353.

Haddon, Mark. *The Curious Incident of the Dog in the Night-Time.* Jeff Woodman, narrator. Prince Frederick, MD: Recorded Books, 2003.

Harris, Karen. Review of *Mr. Paradise,* by Elmore Leonard, Robert Forster, narrator. *Booklist* 100 (April 15, 2004): 1450.

Hartshorn, Laurie. Review of *The Story of Edgar Sawtelle,* by David Wroblewski, Richard Poe, narrator. *Booklist* 105 (December 15, 2009): 86.

Hooper, Brad. Review of *Cars: A Celebration,* by Quentin Willson. *Booklist* 98 (September 15, 2001): 173.

Kirn, Walter. "Lexical Overdrive." Review of *Demonology,* by Rick Moody. *New York Times Book Review* (February 25, 2001): 12–13.

———. "Serious Trouble: John Barth Returns—Not for the Better." Review of *Coming Soon!!!* by John Barth. *GQ* (November 2001): 204.

Knoblauch, Mark. Review of *Comfort Me with Apples: More Adventures at the Table,* by Ruth Reichl. *Booklist* 97 (April 1, 2001): 1427.

Lane, Anthony. *Nobody's Perfect.* New York: Knopf, 2002.

"*Marie Antoinette: The Journey,* by Antonia Fraser." "Briefly Noted," *New Yorker* (September 24, 2001): 93.

McCay, Mary. Review of *Revolutionary Road,* by Richard Yates, Mark Bramhall, narrator. *Booklist* 105 (April 1, 2009): 72.

Mitchell, Margaret. *Gone with the Wind.* New York: Macmillan, 1936.

Pitt, David. Review of *The Bodies Left Behind,* by Jeffery Deaver, Holter Graham, narrator. *Booklist* 105 (March 1, 2009): 69.

Price, Reynolds. *The Promise of Rest.* New York: Atheneum, 1995.

Prose, Francine. "The Bones of Muzhiks." Review of *The Complete Works of Isaac Babel,* by Isaac Babel. *Harper's Magazine* 303 (November 2001): 74–79.

Saricks, Joyce. Review of *It's in His Kiss,* by Julia Quinn, Simon Prebble, narrator. *Booklist* 103 (September 15, 2006): 76.

Smith, Candace. Review of *The Book of Night Women,* by Marion James, Robin Miles, narrator. *Booklist* 105 (April 15, 2009): 58.

Updike, John. *Due Considerations.* New York: Knopf, 2007.

———. *Hugging the Shore.* New York: Knopf, 1983.

Wagner, Erica. "Expatriate Game." Review of *Lulu in Marrakech,* by Diane Johnson. *New York Times Book Review* (October 26, 2008): 8.

Welty, Eudora. *A Writer's Eye: Collected Book Reviews.* Jackson, MS: University Press of Mississippi, 1994.

Wilkens, Mary Frances. Review of *Hide,* by Lisa Gardner, Maggie-Meg Reed, narrator. *Booklist* 103 (May 1, 2007): 50.

Wyatt, Neal. Review of *The Good Earth,* by Pearl S. Buck, Anthony Heald, narrator. *Booklist* 104 (December 1, 2007): 65.

———. Review of *To Kill a Mockingbird,* by Harper Lee, Sissy Spacek, narrator. *Booklist* 103 (December 1, 2006): 70.

INDEX

You may also be interested in

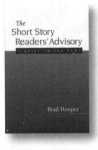

The Short Story Readers' Advisory: In this comprehensive reference, you'll find an introduction to the world of short story writing, more than 200 critical essays covering short story writers past and present, and a step-by-step guide on how to interview readers in order to match their tastes with stories.

The Back Page: Where else can you find an entertaining book filled with the miscellany of the publishing world? Readers can discover everything from the trivial to the important in Bill Ott's *The Back Page,* part readers' advisory and part commentary on the world of books and literature, good and not so good.

Writing and Publishing: If you are interested in writing or reviewing for the library community or in publishing a book, or if you need to write and publish for tenure, then *Writing and Publishing* is for you. This book includes practical how-to guidance covering fiction, poetry, children's books/magazines, self-publishing, literary agents, personal blogging, and other topics.

The Readers' Advisory Guide to Genre Fiction, Second Edition: Provocative and spirited, this guide offers hands-on strategies for librarians who want to become experts at figuring out what their readers are seeking and how to match books with those interests.